HOW TO LEAD A CORPORATE SPIN-OFF

LEDA CSANKA

HOW TO LEAD A CORPORATE SPIN-OFF

The Tech Leader's Survival Guide to a Strategic Divestiture

LEDA CSANKA

By Leda Csanka

© Copyright

How to Lead a Corporate Spin-Off

The Tech Leader's Survival Guide to a Strategic Divestiture

1st Edition. 2018

ASIN: (Amazon Kindle) B07DHY138W

ISBN: (Ingram Spark) PAPERBACK **978-1-7326071-1-8**

ISBN: (Ingram Spark) HARDCOVER **978-1-7326071-0-1**

ISBN: (Smashwords) **9780463623701**

ISBN: (Amazon Print) **9781790145553**

CONTACT THE AUTHOR:

Business Name: Leda Csanka Transformative Coaching, Strategic Tech Consulting, LLC

Email: leda.csanka@gmail.com

Phone: 1-866-994-9244

Author Website: www.ledacsanka.com

Business Website: www.strategictechconsulting.com

Book Website: www.howtoleadacorporatespinoff.com

LinkedIn: https://www.linkedin.com/in/lcsanka/

Twitter: https://twitter.com/LedaCsanka

Facebook: https://www.facebook.com/LedaCsankaTransformativeCoaching/

Book Bonus: www.howtoleadacorporatespinoff.com/bonuses

Bonus Materials

Bonus Chapter

When a team has excellent communication and the right culture, it permeates the whole organization, creating a positive and highly functional environment. These two topics are each covered in detail in the chapters of this book.

I am offering you a free downloadable copy of the chapter: *Fostering Excellent Communication* as a sample of the lessons you will learn in the rest of this book. The chapter addresses seven (well, really eight) communication characteristics that when put in place, sow the seeds for an approachable, inclusive, and high-functioning workplace.

Click here for information on how to access your free chapter: **www.howtoleadacorporatespinoff.com.**

Bonus Videos

I am providing bonus videos of some material in the book to further clarify that information. These videos help bring the topics into a very engaging format. My intention is to develop this bonus content over time as a growing library and resource for you. Check the site regularly for the most recent additions.

Click here to access bonus videos:

www.howtoleadacorporatespinoff.com/bonuses.

Contact Me

I am also available for consulting and coaching on organizational change, strategic review and planning, vendor research and selection support, and overall program management.

You can reach me directly at **Leda.Csanka@gmail.com.**

Find my full contact information on the copyright page.

Table of Contents

Program Management

Production Ready

Pacing

Conclusion

Introduction

Congratulations on Your Opportunity!

Before we begin, let me first congratulate you. I am assuming that if you have found this book, or if it has found its way to you, then you are about to embark on a remarkable career opportunity that doesn't come around very often—once in a career or lifetime, if you are lucky!

I am assuming that you are the senior technology leader or one of the senior members of a leadership team and you have either just learned that your division is for sale or that it has already been sold. If you are farther along the process of divestiture or spin-off, *How to Lead a Corporate Spin-Off* can provide practical support for you too. The lessons are not just intended to support you as you cut the cord from your legacy parent firm. They also are meant to help as you go forward with your team and organization into a successful production go-live.

The breadth and scope of a corporate spin-off and divestiture are vast. If your firm is typical of this kind of effort, many of the IT services that are provided to your division are delivered from the parent company in the form of shared services. Now that you are about to be sold, or spun-off, it is your responsibility to replace these services and stand up your firm as an independent organization.

The path from application manager or division head to chief information or technology officer isn't always an easy one. You are now the decision-maker or at least the one responsible for the final recommendations for all things information technology (IT) at the new company.

This path can feel both exciting and a little overwhelming at the same time. It's also a position that can feel isolated and lonely as you might not be sure where to turn for coaching, support, and help. That's where *How to Lead a Corporate Spin-Off* comes in . . .

Your Roadmap, Playbook, and Set of Reminders

Expect this book to serve as your roadmap, playbook, and set of reminders that you can pull out and review from time to time to center yourself and your team. With *How to Lead a Corporate Spin-Off*, you won't feel isolated or alone on your new journey.

My goal is for this book to come to you early enough in the process to help you make some excellent critical decisions and prepare you for the journey ahead! If I can provide a few key tips, ideas, and strategies to help you to grow into your opportunity with grace, confidence, and success, then I will have fulfilled my purpose in writing this book, in which I share the stories and lessons I learned in the two corporate spin-offs that I headed.

While *How to Lead a Corporate Spin-Off* doesn't contain a secret sauce, a set of silver bullets, or even a magic wand, you can certainly view it as a handbook developed from what I call "Leda's School of Hard Knox." You'll find my story woven throughout the chapters, relating how I grew from a middle manager in a huge insurance company to chief information officer (CIO) overnight and the struggles and lessons I learned along the way. There were some things I got right; some were by design and others purely by luck. Some of my decisions were critical early on and set the tone for success later. You'll also hear about some of the mistakes I made along the way. I hope that by sharing them, I will be able to help you avoid making the same mistakes on your journey.

With *How to Lead a Corporate Spin-Off*, you'll find that you and your team are not alone in this spin-off, but rather, you have the practical advice of someone who has navigated this path before you to guide you. I've both led and participated in not just one divestiture/spin-off—but two. One as a CIO and a full-time employee and the second as an independent consultant who came out of retirement to help lead the second group through the harrowing last five months of their effort that had gotten a little off-track.

The spirit in *How to Lead a Corporate Spin-Off* is (1) to package the crucial information in a way that will coach you through decisions that are likely new for you and (2) to remind you of things you already know but might be overlooking as a result of feeling that excitement—and possibly a bit of the overwhelm—that comes when first learning that you are the leader of the new organization being created from the corporate spin-off.

I want to support you on your way to success as the new chief information officer for your company, and I want to help you hit a home run as you prepare, plan, build your team, and learn the ropes on how to ready the organization for production as a standalone company. I want to see and hear of your successes (you'll find my contact info at the end of the copyright page) as you also learn to pace yourself and avoid the burnout that often brings the tenure of the CIO/CTO to a short end. (To learn more about the potential for burnout I faced in the two spin-offs I led, be sure to check out the About the Author section of this book.)

How to Lead a Corporate Spin-Off: About the Set-Up

I have broken this book down into the following five sections:

1—Prepare: Planning and Partners

If you are in the early stages of your project, then you will get the most out of this section. It supplies information on how to plan for the spin-off effort. It's often hardest to know how to get started. We will discuss the importance of having strategic partners on your team and setting the right strategy. I'll share many of the decision criteria that you'll need to consider as you look at what types of partners are right for you and how to evaluate and select them for success.

2—People

You will likely have a team of people that you have been working with at the parent company for a number of years. These people have had a critical role in the success of the firm to date. Many of them will also be dealing with new opportunities and growth, just as you are. However, not all of them will be able to step into these new challenges. This section gives you some food for thought on how to think about your team and how to lead them through this kind of effort. I lay out how setting and creating the right culture and communication strategies positions your team for success.

3—Program Management

This isn't the same old project you have run for years. There are so many aspects to this kind of effort. This section helps you think about how to break the spin-off into a set of workstreams and to think of the spin-off effort as a program. We will discuss ways to reduce risk, how to respond to things that will go wrong along the way, and the kind of support you might expect from the legacy parent company.

4—Production Ready

This isn't just a one-time project effort, as in—one and done, you are separated. You are building a new company, so you need to think about structuring the organization for success after the separation/spin-off project. You need to create all new operational procedures and processes for your organization. You can leverage best practices from ITIL, but you have to make things appropriately right-sized for your firm. Overall, a spirit of thinking about organizational readiness as an exercise in change management will be a critical success factor.

5—Pacing

"This is a marathon, Leda, not a sprint," was one of the most powerful words of advice I have ever received. Still, after 4.5 years in the role, even with the benefit of this advice, I did get burnt out. I hope to shed light in the area of pacing to help you be aware of this risk of burnout. Not only for yourself, but for all members of your organization. It's a long road ahead, and it takes the whole team to be successful. This section aims to get all of you to the finish line together!

Mostly *How to Lead a Corporate Spin-Off* is for you. I hope you find it worth the quick read that it is intended to be. If you'd like help early on setting your strategy, or you need someone to review your plan, please reach out to me for support and advice. I am available for both consulting assignments and on retainer as an executive coach and advisor. You will find my contact information on the copyright page.

I am providing you with bonus videos of some material in the book to further clarify the information. These bonuses help bring the topics into a more engaging format. My intention is to develop this bonus content over time as a growing library and resource for you. Check the website regularly for the most recent additions.

Click here to access bonus videos:
www.howtoleadacorporatespinoff.com/bonuses.

I hope your journey is filled with excitement, growth, success, and feelings of fulfillment and achievement! Again, congratulations, enjoy the process, and know you aren't alone!

About the Author

Hi. This is Leda Csanka. I want to share with you a little more information about my personal story and how I came to write this book. I know it might seem a little unorthodox for a chief information officer to share a personal story about her own life, goals, and dreams. I appreciate that we are a dry, boring group as a broad generalization, and I have had my fair share of admissions that I have workaholic tendencies like the "next guy." However, if you choose to read this section of the book, perhaps I can help a few of you be successful and not make a couple of the big mistakes I've made in my life.

Ah-Ha!

One day, in 1983, I was sitting in chemistry class, pondering the meaning of life. I had no ambition and no idea what to do with my life. I was sixteen years old and a junior in high school. I hadn't thought a minute about going to college. That was just something we never discussed in my family or even dreamed about. My mother had her own business, and my father was the assistant manager at a grocery store. We lived comfortably. There was a fleeting moment in eighth grade when I thought I wanted to be a veterinarian, but once I learned that it required going to school for more than eight years, I was like, "Forget that!"

I sat there daydreaming or escaping, whichever word you'd like to use, when our teacher Mr. B started discussing computer programming. He began talking about how in Connecticut most of the industry was insurance and how they all needed computer programmers. My ears perked up. He continued, "You can go to school just two miles from here at Waterbury State Technical College, get a degree in programming in just two years, and then have a full-time career making $18,000 a year."

"Eighteen thousand dollars a year. Wow, that's unbelievable. I'll be able to move out of my parents' place, live on my own, and even buy my own house! I could be my own person and live the way I'd like to!" I thought to myself. It seemed like the ultimate freedom!

My drive for independence is probably a story that many of us have, but the desire to be a computer programmer? I honestly hadn't even seen a computer before. My only experience with a computer was the one used to shrink people in the film *The Incredible Shrinking Woman*. However, I was sold. I knew it was the path for me.

I started technical school in September 1984, having never touched a computer, but somehow I loved it! Thankfully! I was good at programming. My friends all needed tutoring. I ended up helping many of them by writing their programs. I would do each assignment three or four different ways. I found it easy, and I didn't realize helping all my friends was just giving me more confidence.

I realized that the two-year program wouldn't be enough, and I created a plan to go to the University of Connecticut right after graduating. As a transfer student, I started the management information systems degree in the business school. Things just fell into place for me there as well. I was semesters ahead of my peer group in the computer classes, so I became a teaching assistant and made some money helping other students, grading programs, etc.

After 4.5 years of school, I graduated with two degrees and entered the workforce. I lived at home with my parents for two years. In 1991 I purchased my first home at twenty-four years old. I was finally on my own.

It was around this time that Tony Robbins was on the late-night infomercials selling his Personal Power 30-Day CD program. I invested the $300 or so for the CDs. From that point on, I was on a mission. Tony told us to write down all of our goals. I was excited! He urged, "Make them seem impossible!" So I did. I wrote down, at twenty-four years old, that I wanted to be a CIO of a company and live on the beach in California.

I then spent the next twenty years doing everything I could to achieve that goal. I won't take you through all the steps; just know that I had a mission, I had a drive, and I worked hard. I worked a LOT. I spent all my energy, and the number one priority in my life was to achieve this dream.

Another Ah-Ha!

Fast-forward to June 2016, twenty-five years later: I had everything I had ever wanted. I had achieved everything on that "Tony Robbins' List." I was walking on the beach, in California, CTO of a company. That's when I realized that I was completely unfulfilled. I lost out on and missed out on the meaning of life. I was having fun and joy while I was working towards those dreams, but somehow life didn't seem as great as I had always envisioned it would be.

I had spent the last six years or so as an executive and led my team through a very difficult spin-off. I'd worked several mergers and acquisitions, and helped to grow the company significantly, but

I still felt like something was missing. I decided that day on my long walk on the beach, mile seven of a ten-mile walk, that I needed to retire and figure out this thing called life.

I was forty-nine. Retired! Woo-hoo! Right? Well, it wasn't so easy. I realized that I had neglected my relationship, neglected my friends, and neglected my family. I had no hobbies other than reading technical or business books, and I had allowed myself to put on thirty pounds by eating and drinking too much to manage my stress and to numb my issues.

I have done some serious soul-searching in the last two years. I've made some new friends, but my marriage was a casualty of my bad choices around priorities. I've spent time at the Chopra Center and had an amazing spiritual awakening that inspired me to become a meditation instructor with them. I've started to read the Bible and study religions of the world.

Mostly what I've learned is that life is about more than work and about more than trying to get ahead. I understand that we all need to feed our family, maybe feed our egos, but I found out that life is about learning what feeds your soul.

After years of working for "food" both to feed my family and my ego, I've learned that teaching, coaching, and helping others is what I am passionate about.

New and Inspired

I am re-entering the workforce, but in a new and inspired way. I have become a certified professional coach, and I am creating workshops to help people find balance and create visions for their lives that won't leave them feeling burnt out. I teach meditation classes online, and I decided to start re-engaging with corporate America.

I have a message. I have a purpose. I hope that my experience at leading two companies through divestitures and spin-offs will let me find both speaking engagements and consulting work. I want to help other executives, not just technical leaders, realize there is more to life than getting ahead in the corporate world.

We can achieve, we can dream, we can aspire! However, I want to help others do it in a way that doesn't result in burnout. I want to help business leaders avoid the two-year cycle of spinning that I've just gone through and figure out what makes them happy and what brings them joy. I want to support them on the quest to find career fulfillment and a balanced personal life.

As I write this book, I've moved from my beach house into a small cabin in the woods in Idyllwild, California. I am going through a divorce that is my fault from years of neglect and having the wrong priorities. However, I am building a new life and creating a new vision and future for myself! Life is exciting again.

Today is day two back on the hill after being evacuated for five days after the Cranston fire. Our town was saved by the bravery of the firefighters from all over California who battled the fire set by an arsonist. The town is starting to hustle and bustle. People are meeting at the post office and in groups in the market to talk about each of our experiences during the evacuation. We are healing and supporting each other.

I look at the love, support, and generosity of the human spirit that I see here in the forest each day and realize that I was missing out on the simple things in life.

I want to help you achieve all you've been dreaming of. I want to see you thrive! Mostly, I want to help you do this without losing yourself, or burning out.

We all have lives to live, inside *and* outside of the office.

I hope this book saves you from having to go through some of the pain I've been through, so you won't need to learn the hard way.

My "Official" Bio

For those of you interested in my "official" bio, without my personal story, here it is:

Leda Csanka has spent more than thirty years in technology and the financial services industry, ten of those years as a CIO, CTO, and independent consultant/business owner. She has successfully led two corporate spin-offs to become IT organizations for standalone companies. Her first opportunity to drive one of these efforts was as a newly "minted" CIO promoted from middle management at ING and selected to be one of twelve executives asked to sell and lead three of the broker/dealer firms through the sale and divestiture process. The second time around leading a spin-off, Leda was a seasoned executive turned independent consultant leveraging her experience to bring best practices to the effort.

Her passion is to share the lessons of technology leadership from the perspective of someone who learned the hard way, in day-to-day combat in the trenches, with the team, successfully executing hundreds of projects through shifting priorities and the changing demands of the corporate world.

Her book *How to Lead a Corporate Spin-Off* reached number one international bestseller status within forty-eight hours of being published on Amazon. Leda is a speaker, consultant, and executive coach available to help you and your managers transform your organization through change. Her experience can help you by having a trusted advisor available as your partner. You don't need to tackle your next big project alone.

Leda has a program management background and has been responsible for leading programs as large as $35 million and up to

150 people across multiple physical locations. She has extensive experience in staffing and creating teams to implement strategic projects and a proven ability to lead the strategic planning and technical road-mapping process for a 900-employee organization.

Since retiring from corporate positions in mid-2016, Leda has started her own consulting company, Strategic Tech Consulting and an executive and transformational coaching practice. Her latest passion is teaching people how to meditate as a primordial sound meditation instructor with the Chopra Center.

To contact Leda, you can find her contact information on the copyright page of this book.

PREPARE: PLANNING AND PARTNERS

1.

Your Firm Has Been
Sold, Now What?

If you are at the very beginning of the spin-off process, you might be wondering how to get started on the journey. The firm is for sale or has already sold, and you have been named either the chief technology officer or chief information officer of the new entity. Now, what do you do?

First, don't panic! Those first few moments of doubt do go away! However, if your path is anything like mine was, the feelings of isolation and self-doubt can creep back up from time to time. Just know that this is a journey and period of tremendous growth. It's exciting!

The best way I know how to help you is to share from my own experiences. In describing my experiences with corporate spin-offs—remember, I've worked through two—I will highlight the steps and best practices that my team and I took. These should serve as a great game plan for you as well.

The first separation project that I led started out a little overwhelming. When I understood that I was entrusted to lead my team and replicate all IT services to create an independent, standalone company, I had a moment of panic. A senior leader at the legacy parent firm called to inform me that I'd need to figure out how to "spin off" the firm. This was the first I was learning about the spin-off and my role in it.

After the call, I noticed that I had stopped breathing. I took a few deep breaths. Next, I said to myself, "This is my moment. I need to show up and rise to the occasion." I allowed myself just a moment of doubt, insecurity, and skepticism, and then I got down to business. I asked myself, "What would I do if I knew how to get started?" From there, I just started moving forward, making decisions based on the culmination of all I had learned over the years. Here are the four big initial steps I recommend you take.

First—Define the Scope of Services

Your first step is to define the services that are currently being provided by the parent company. This will help you identify the overall scope of your project.

For the first spin-off effort I was involved with, the parent company provided us with all IT capabilities, except for application development and production support of the applications used to run our specific business unit. Everything else was from shared services at the parent.

The scope of your effort can be as broad as this example, or even as simple as just taking over all the vendor contracts. It will depend on how integrated you are with the legacy firm.

Second—Evaluate the Skills on Your Team

As you define your scope of services, you should also lay out the skills required to support those services. For services that will be new for you and your team, you will find yourself identifying new roles altogether. These actions begin the process of determining which members of the team you should be asking to come with your organization, and they will help you to define a "hiring list" of the roles that you will need to fill.

My first effort at creating a list of services to build included corporate applications, like payroll and the general ledger, all hardware, and software used by employees, a data center, and infrastructure management. The list of services continued with telephone, security, networking, centralized vendor management and contracting, help desk services, email, internet and intranet sites, etc. I started to look at both my skills and experiences and those of my team. If we were going to provide all these services to the new organization on our own going forward, we needed to broaden the technical expertise we had on hand quickly. These domains were a bit different than the experience of the application development team identified as the resources that would be spun off.

At this stage, our list of gaps was much longer than our list of strengths.

Third—Take an Honest Assessment of Your Leadership Gaps

As exciting as this opportunity is and as ready as you think you are, you need to take an honest assessment of your strengths and weaknesses.

In my own first few weeks, the gap I was most concerned with was my lack of experience as a CIO. In the past, I had run both large programs and teams, but I had never run all of information technology for a company. I knew about all these domain areas as the leader of an IT department that worked in partnership with other IT organizations to provide these services for my business unit.

However, I wasn't experienced in the day-to-day operations and management required to run a standalone company. Due to my fear of failure in this new position, I felt great pressure to try and close my gaps first.

To accomplish this, I spent a significant amount of time on weekends researching and learning about all facets of IT. I wanted to understand more about trends and how to establish a security policy. I wanted to get a sense of the different vendors and services available in the industry. I laid out a series of critical success factors by which I anticipated being judged. I worried mostly about how to gain respect and credibility, both from my team, the other executives, and industry leaders of the other firms. Dealing with my insecurities about my technical competencies brought up a tremendous fear: "I am in this alone."

Only now, as the Monday morning quarterback, do I realize that, of course, I wasn't alone. There were a lot of people who contributed to the effort's success. There is tremendous truth to the words, "It takes a village." Fortunately, it did not take me long to realize there was just too much to try and learn on my own. With the amount of work on the horizon, this wasn't something I would be able to overcome by throwing myself into it. Pure brute force and a will to succeed wouldn't cut it this time. Yes, I needed to throw myself into it, but the effort was frankly just too big.

I set up a series of sessions with my senior team and talked loosely about the effort ahead of us. They were allowed to know that we were up for sale, but they couldn't know any of the details of our future state. I was able to include them in some of the early planning by talking about potential future scenarios and scenario planning. I was able to use the case of a "standalone company" to discuss with everyone, both in a group setting and through a series of one-on-one interviews with each of them, to probe our team's depth.

We were a small division of a huge company, and the experience that we had on our team, other than application development, was almost ten years dated regarding managing and running hardware and infrastructure teams. Many of us had been application development managers our entire careers and never had the pleasure of running infrastructure services before.

Knowing that we were still short on experience and long on needs, my first reaction was to start calling around my contacts at the legacy parent company and asking those peers across the firm what they thought I should do. I knew we should leverage their expertise and get ideas on approaches, consultants that we could use, or firms we might work with to tackle this kind of effort.

After only a few phone calls to what I had always felt was my extended team at the parent company, I received a candid call from a member of their executive management team. I was told that it was a liability for anyone to give me information, and they had all been instructed not to help us define our strategy or approach in any way. "Sorry, Leda, you are on your own."

Fourth—Build Your Support Team

Although I felt more alone than ever, on your project you can avoid this situation and feeling from the minute you start! The best approach is to find a consulting firm to help you define your scope and set your overall strategy. Ideally, hire a consulting firm experienced at finding other consulting firms!

In my first spin-off, our most significant gap was to identify how to convert and mobilize a data center and get some seed money to begin a project to find a data center partner. Your priorities will likely be different based on your set of services and the skill gaps you identify, but finding your initial support team is critical. You will be pleased to discover that there is a niche vendor for everything. If you can describe what you are looking for, there is someone who has done it already and who can help you.

Don't be paralyzed by not knowing what to do or having the expertise yourself. In the initial moments of panic and self-doubt, you need to have the courage to step forth, create a game plan, and start to execute. The first few moves you make are watched and evaluated, not only by your team but also by the other executives and potential buyers/investors.

The time is now. This is your moment. You need to show up.

Finding strategic partners and hiring experts who have done this before is your best first move!

I mentioned this before, but it's worth repeating here as well. If you'd like help early on setting your strategy, or you need someone to review your plan, please reach out to me for support and advice. I am available for both consulting assignments and on retainer as an executive coach and advisor. You will find my contact information on the copyright page.

Up Next

We're going to be looking at your strategic partner strategy and addressing pressing issues like in-house support vs. managed services, single vs. multiple vendors, and the cloud vs. dedicated platforms.

2.

Define Your Strategic
Partner Strategy

A s you review the scope of services that you will need to build and the list of gaps of both roles and skillsets that you need to hire for, you'll need to prioritize and strategize your attack plan. The researching of vendors, the process of staffing open positions, and the interviewing of potential partners makes for a time-consuming process. If you aren't careful, it can drag down both you and your team. This chapter delivers insights and strategies to help you during this trying time, so—hopefully—it will be *less* trying!

Research *Just Enough*

Research is very time-consuming, and you will quickly find it gets a bit overwhelming. If you have a team that includes other leaders, I suggest you divide and conquer rather than taking on too much of this yourself. Try to get approval to bring in others on the effort as quickly as possible. They will likely be required to sign a non-disclosure agreement (NDA), but you need to scale this activity fast. You need to get yourself educated *just enough* to make the right decisions. Even as you hire consultants to help make recommendations, you will need to be confident in what they are proposing.

In-House Support vs. Managed Services

As you review the list of IT services that your team needs to deliver to the whole of the new organization, you need to ask yourself if you want to (1) build the services in-house and hire people to both build and support them for you, or (2) hire a firm to provide managed services.

For every organization and group of people, there will be a different right answer here. The capabilities of your staff, the level of services that you have been autonomously providing already, and the time you have to become independent will all be factors. There won't be a single answer or strategy that works for all services. For example, it's common to think about using Microsoft O365 instead of implementing Exchange servers for email. If you have a local onsite help desk and desktop support personnel, then you might be in a position to support this entirely in-house.

I recommend that you put together a strategy for each of the IT services independent of each other. There will be pros and cons for each. Consequently, documenting them for each approach will force you and the support team you've built to at least have a structured dialogue around each decision.

Both of the spin-off projects I was part of heavily leveraged managed services due to the urgency and time-to-market requirements to separate from the parent firms. Each effort decided that the respective organizations would be best served if their infrastructure services strategy were a managed service strategy, putting vendor management as the skillset required internally, rather than the technical competency and expertise related to standing up infrastructure services themselves. This strategy positioned each organization for a higher probability of meeting the availability SLAs (service level agreements) required both by the business and external clients. This also reduced the staffing efforts needed to find and attract talented people to manage these functions in-house.

Single vs. Multiple Vendors

One of the critical decisions you should address early on is whether to partner with a single firm that has multiple competencies or multiple vendors with different niche focus areas.

I've had the opportunity to work with both models, and I typically recommend using multiple vendors rather than finding one vendor willing to sign up to support everything. I will share the pros and cons of each option below. Let me reiterate: any decision you make is right only for a point in time and a specific set of circumstances.

One of the benefits of using multiple vendors is that you can use the best-of-breed strategy in selecting the right partner for each of the services or capabilities. This approach doesn't mean that you won't find vendors that are willing to bundle services together or ones that come to the table with a recommended third-party partner they utilize. It just means that you have a lot of flexibility and choice. In my experience, it's best not only to have a partner with expertise at implementing a service or installing a system, but also one that has experience at running that service in a production environment. There are many ongoing operational processes and procedures to build, and this part of the implementation plan often is overlooked. I have a dedicated chapter on this activity later in the book to help you avoid underestimating the amount of work involved. A partner who has run these services as a managed service or as a production organization brings experience and best practices to the table, which helps to prevent a lot of issues later on when incidents occur after go live.

The second benefit of multiple vendors doesn't become apparent right away; it usually surfaces during the project execution. We will discuss program management a little later, but you will be implementing these services and capabilities as a set of projects executed in parallel. As the activities progress, it is possible that you will be dealing with issues on different parts of the program at the same time. If you have a multi-partner strategy, working to resolve those issues concurrently is less of a resource drain on your partners when you need to escalate to the highest levels of support within their firm. Also, it creates overall less contention within any single vendor.

If you use a single vendor to implement and support too many services and you do find yourself dealing with issues in different domain areas at the same time, the tensions tend to get high as you escalate within different arms of the vendor. Not only can this erode the partnership, but you may be inadvertently in a situation where the partner is diverting resources and technical expertise at the expense of one part of the project for another. In cases when this does occur, you can anticipate the compounding, unintended effect and consequence of project delays in more than one area. I liken this approach to "having too many eggs in one basket."

The downside to managing multiple partners is that there is extra work involved. It requires relationship-building with the management within each firm and knowing how to navigate different processes. Your team needs to deal with multiple account managers and support groups, and it necessitates a formal vendor management process that is consistent across the various vendors. The operational procedures that you will need to establish, like incident management and change management, become more complicated.

It's not my recommendation that you define a hard-and-fast single vs. multiple vendor strategy. I think that your initial research should include vendors of both capabilities. I recommend starting with this approach because you might find a single vendor that does everything except for one niche area and you decide there is a perfect smaller vendor to do that one thing.

Cloud vs. Dedicated Platforms

You will need a strategy and position on whether you are open to using cloud applications and services or you require physically-dedicated infrastructure and services. In some industries, the risk of cloud services and the security overhead needing to feel safe in that kind of environment may be a big influencer. Try to lay out your position and strategy on this early; it will likely come into your decision-making processes and selection criteria when you evaluate vendors.

Up Next

We're not done with considering strategic partners. In this chapter, I gave some important areas of consideration to help you set your strategy and determine your organization's approach. Next up is reviewing more criteria for selecting partners and outside firms.

3.

Establish Selection Criteria
for Vendors/Partners

Once you have set your strategy and determined an approach for your organization, you will need to establish partner selection criteria, create a scorecard, and design a process to evaluate potential firms. You will have many technical and functional requirements. These need to be documented in a request for proposal (RFP) to send to the different candidates.

Your team is likely using a custom-built vendor assessment scorecard, and you're going to follow a vendor assessment process. If your team doesn't have one that you've used before, the strategy of hiring a vendor to find other vendors will be perfect. You can hire someone with experience at vendor selection, and they will have a scorecard they've used before. If you are executing this part of the project on your own, there are many examples of scorecards on the internet you can use. Most are Excel templates that list all your requirements as rows in a spreadsheet, and you weight each requirement for importance. Each vendor will be asked to respond to your RFP, and I recommend that they present, in person, their proposals.

There are several other decision criteria beyond technical requirements for you to consider when analyzing the different types of firms. Let's look at those now.

Size of Firm and Breadth of Services

The size of firms with experience to support you varies significantly. You will find both niche, independent consultants who have done this exact type of project before and large, traditional IT outsourcing firms that have seen many different kinds of projects.

Many of the traditional, large firms are experts at providing infrastructure to other organizations as a managed service. They have project managers available to run your conversion project and architects on staff to help design and engineer your environment. They can help with a broad range of technical decisions: the right size and type of hardware, the size and speed of the pipe required for the amount of data you will be transporting, good predictions about the storage requirements for your firm, and accurate projections for your future growth needs. Their expertise will be critical for designing an environment that provides the right level of availability and disaster-recovery needs to your organization.

These larger firms are experienced at providing all these services, and they come to the table with "their way" of doing things, a set of standard processes. They can help with all aspects of the project ahead of you: planning, preparing, designing, building, implementing, ongoing management, and daily care and feeding of all things related to the service. A full-service option is a great approach when your team has little experience or time to build out these skills in-house. However, it comes with a larger cost and can be very expensive. These are tradeoffs that only you and your team/firm can decide. I like the approach of building "right-size IT" because you may not need all the services that come bundled with a large firm's full-service management.

On the other end of the scale, you can find infrastructure firms that provide only "ping, power, and pipe." You are essentially renting space in their facility, and they offer redundant electrical power supply to your equipment and secured access in and out of the facility to the internet. In these types of arrangements, your team either provides all other services or you separately hire infrastructure consultants in addition to the space provider to help with the planning, building, maintaining, etc., as needed to supplement your team.

There are many middle positions to take between these two ends of the spectrum. I've seen several companies tackle building out the infrastructure themselves with the help of infrastructure consultants and full-time staff. Then they hire local "hands and feet" with access to the data center and equipment to physically restart or replace hardware if that's needed. There is a wide variety of options.

As a general rule, the larger a firm is, the greater the number of employees they have on staff and the more expertise within their organization to call in for unique situations or issues that can arise. However, access to talent and knowledge isn't the only thing to consider when looking at the size of the partner company. One of the common mistakes I've seen over the years is the misconception that you will have more leverage over a partner based on the size of the contract you are negotiating, and, therefore, you falsely assume it is always to your benefit to bundle as many services together in a single deal.

Many leaders think it's all about negotiation power, and you can demand lower prices expecting higher volume discounts and build in price breaks for growth if you purchase all your hardware from a single provider. However, the other side of the argument is that if you spread the investment around to multiple providers, then if something goes wrong during the contract period, it's a lot easier to replace the hundred-thousand-dollar vendor than it is to exit a multi-million-dollar multi-year contract. High termination fees and difficult exit clauses can make it difficult to execute a back-out plan.

Reach and Depth

During the project, there is a high probability that issues will surface, and you will need to lean on your partner for expertise and resources to resolve the problems. As I mentioned, with larger firms, there are likely experts somewhere within their company to help solve the issue even if those resources are not on your account. A firm that is right-size for you will be one that is willing to divert resources from other areas of their firm to your account to overcome any show-stopper issues. You want a firm that has enough depth and expertise in-house to support you.

It's not just access to technical expertise that's needed, though. If the vendor isn't large enough, there are potential leadership issues as well. A strategy that relies on a single vendor to do everything can be detrimental depending on the size of their company. A firm that is too small may have only a few senior leaders. These leaders are often spread too thin across multiple accounts, so getting their focus and attention in times of crisis can be difficult.

Right-Size Partnership with Skin in the Game

The goal is to find vendors that are the right size for you. You need to look at the number of employees they have in their organization, the number of clients they have with the specific service or activity you are hiring them for, and the number of active projects they have on their plate. You also need an understanding of their organization's structure, and you should know the track record of their leadership team.

For our team, finding a niche consulting firm to help with our highest-priority gap of planning for and executing the data center conversion strategy, defining the security architecture, and building out the data center managed service was relatively easy. These types of services were available from all the large IT outsourcing firms, but we found a firm that was just about the same size as our firm. They were a young, growing company and had a team with hands-on experience in designing, architecting, and managing data center conversion projects. We hired our initial partner to help us find the more strategic partnerships we needed for the longer term. We decided on a mid-size company that provided all managed services as it related to the data center as well.

One of the primary deciding factors for us was that we didn't want to be a small fish in a giant pond. With a company that was so large that, once we went live, our little infrastructure footprint wouldn't get much of their management's attention and our voice would be lost if incidents occurred. This fear was a concern for the initial data center build-out project as well. As time-to-market became the most critical factor for us, having a voice if the project started having issues meeting dates and timeframes seemed to be most important.

The downside is that the growth strategy of a mid-size company can make them a likely target of an acquisition in their own right, and that ultimately happened to the firm we selected. Luckily, it happened after our conversion and go-live.

If you do select a larger firm as your ultimate provider, there are a few things you can do in the contracting step as you create the statement of work (SOW) for the project that will help to mitigate the risk of not having a voice by being too small. You could include having a "refund or penalty" for not meeting the target timelines that are laid out in the SOW. You could also insist that the team used to implement the project remains on the effort until your new organization has gone live and become stabilized as a production environment for a month or two. Penalties are a great way to accomplish the goal of getting some skin in the game with the success of the effort in a different way.

Once you select a vendor, strategize quickly to find a way to get them to put skin in the game so that the success of the project is a win for them as well as you. It's possible to build partnership incentives into the contract. That could include monetary bonuses for no fallout, incidents, or issues during the first ninety days, or an early implementation. Non-monetary incentives could be the promise to provide testimonials and to attend their annual conference and be on stage as their key client. Planting the seed for future projects and the commitment to be a reference go a long way. You could be their flagship client and someone who advocates for their firm going forward by offering to be part of a case study and promising to speak at their events and conferences. In this way, you may be able to gain a closer-knit partnership early on. This approach worked well for us, and our project would not have been a success without the right commitment from our partners.

"Current-State" Expertise

Another aspect to your decision-making efforts is to consider the amount of value you might get from the legacy infrastructure provider. For the two separate projects that I was involved with, both of the parent companies provided the infrastructure services to their respective groups by outsourcing the infrastructure to other outsourcing firms. Each was operating in a managed services capacity. In these types of situations, you should consider if establishing a new contract with the current-state provider would get you to market the quickest and if it would be an appropriate option for you.

A legacy provider strategy won't be the best choice if your application portfolio is starting to age and is running on dated and end-of-life hardware. If you have scale or availability needs, you may need to introduce a new architectural design, and now is likely the appropriate time to introduce that. You will need to consider how much application redesign is required to run in a state-of-the-art model and weigh this against a "lift-and-load" approach. When setting up a new data center, you will be purchasing new hardware, and if you haven't made a move to running in a private cloud or on virtual machines, this is the time to do it. Overall, the need for new design and new hardware would eliminate any advantage to the legacy firm.

Our legacy infrastructure provider was invited to participate in our request for proposal (RFP) with other firms of various sizes. Unfortunately for them, their account team assumed they would win the RFP and the business from the beginning, so they showed up very poorly throughout our entire process. They were not the lowest scored vendor in the process, but they were in the bottom percentile. I had hoped that we would find them to be the lowest risk because they had experience with managing our application portfolio already, and we would be lucky and only need to renegotiate the contract as our new entity. However, based on their poor performance through the process, we did select a new infrastructure services firm. This proved to be one of the best decisions we made.

Many executives always go for the lowest-cost provider and assume that their existing provider is the way to achieve that objective. You may be surprised at the expense and the pricing model provided because you could lose the pricing scale you previously enjoyed once you are spun off and on your own. The unitized cost of all hardware, whether it's for the data center or your employees' desktops, goes up when you don't get to take advantage of those volume discounts that you might have been receiving as part of a legacy parent company.

Culture and Fit

So far, we have discussed finding the right-size firm, getting them to put their skin in the game, determining the right set of services for you, and we briefly touched on cost expectations. The next factor to consider is that of culture and fit. This concept is not a "touchy-feely" thing. It is very important.

Leda Csanka

"Fit" is about the people—not just the company and its culture—but the actual people you will have assigned to your team and those you will be working with every day. Sometimes, in this process, they send the A-team to do the sales presentation, but you get the B-, C- or D-team to work with on your project. Make sure that from the start while you are still vetting, you are talking with the actual people who will be assigned to your account, working on your project, and running operations post-go live.

Yes, you do need to ensure that the people have the technical skills and experience you are paying for, but that's not all you are vetting. You are trying to figure out if they have values aligned with your own. Do you get along with them?

These factors are important because no matter how well you get along with people, there are going to be difficulties. Therefore, it's important in your vetting that you try to get a feel for how someone is going to react when issues do surface. I'm not suggesting you need to be best friends with everyone, but that you have enough of a relationship to solve the stressful situations that are ahead. You will need to be able to have a candid, open, and honest dialogue with them, and you need to be able to work together under pressure.

Implementation Management and Transition Support

As things start to align, and you find the perfect partner to manage your infrastructure services for the new standalone model, during the process you should assess their implementation and conversion experience. It is rare that people who are excellent at running IT operations are also good implementers and project managers. Many of the firms will have two separate teams: an implementation/conversion team and a managed service group. The team you run the project with is the conversion team, and the team you will be working with day-to-day post-implementation is the service team. The service team might not be very engaged in the project until the very end when the environment has been built out.

It's necessary that in the vetting stage you meet both teams for firms using the two-team strategy. When you meet them, be sure to ask questions around the transition and handoffs between the two groups. In many firms, the project team is led by different management, and they are being pressured to get off the project as soon as possible. Identifying early that there is a transition period that needs to occur post-implementation is essential. You will want to ensure that there is a level of support available to both the managed service team and to you as the client-customer for at least thirty days after you go live.

Operational Maturity

One area often overlooked when evaluating vendors is understanding the maturity and practices of the day-to-day operations of the managed service team. When you are spinning off to become your own standalone company, your team may not have experience in delivering managed services to the organization. So, you'll need to spend time planning for what day-to-day operations will be like after you are live. I will discuss more about operational readiness later in the book, but for now I want to emphasize that you ensure the firm you select does actually have "live" clients in the service model they are proposing, and they have current customers that you can call for references to help you assess if there are any gaps in their experience. It's okay to select someone in a bundled service mode where one or more of the services is a new delivery item and those operational processes are built for you as part of the project. However, this should be an eyes-wide-open decision for you. A service delivered by an inexperienced firm will create an unplanned drag on the project activities if not carefully accounted for and planned around.

Operational maturity isn't only about their ability to deliver on any one of the services, but also about how they function as a firm overall. I recommend that you add specific questions on operations, similar to the following: "How will you report incidents and outages? What are the procurement processes for additional resources or support? How do you prioritize issues? What kind of ongoing support can we expect from you? Are you willing to provide quarterly scorecards? Do you provide operational reporting out of the gate pertaining to the service level availability (SLA) agreements? How are you doing against those SLAs for other clients?"

Firm Legitimacy

It's essential to call references for the firm and check their financial health to determine if they are viable and sustainable from an operational perspective. This attempts to protect you from a vendor going out of business six months after you sign the contract.

In my spin-off experiences, we also validated our partners with a visit to the website Glassdoor to determine what kind of employer they are and how effective they are at retaining their employees. I also recommend a quick Google search on the company to identify if there are any outstanding lawsuits. If you have a legal or financial team that is part of your procurement process, this is something that team probably does for you. However, your firm may not have these resources or teams built yet, in which case, you will be performing some of this research and vetting. You'll want to determine if the firm is an acquisition target or currently going through an acquisition, so you can understand beforehand if there is a possible distraction for their management team that could prevent them from focusing on supporting you and your effort.

Whether it be helping you in selecting the criteria for your vendor-partners or in problem-solving with you on another aspect of your spin-off effort, I am available. To explore this possibility, you can reach out to me by finding my contact information on the copyright page.

Up Next

Now that you've considered the criteria for selecting partners, in the next chapter, we'll look at four broad categories of vendors and consultants: applications, software, hardware, and services.

4.

Research the Types of Vendors and Consultants Available for Hire

As I mentioned before, there's a partner or vendor for everything. They fall into four broad categories, which I will discuss in more detail in this section: applications, software, hardware, and services.

Applications

These are considered the vendors that provide enterprise applications like enterprise resource planning software, payroll, general ledger, and procurement applications. Examples of companies in this applications category include SAP, Oracle, Sage, Microsoft, Siemens, and Workday. The applications are provided as a cloud service. All support, maintenance, and operations are provided by the vendor as a bundled service.

Software

Software vendors provide licenses to products that you host in-house, or they may provide hosting services for a separate fee as well. This category includes all licensed software that your business users need to perform tasks in the day-to-day functions. Microsoft Office, project management tools, email, collaboration tools, technology monitoring, and development tools are examples of software in this category.

Hardware

Vendors that provide hardware products, like computers, telephones, printers, and mobile devices, fall into this category.

Vendor Application Resellers

Each of the above categories can also be purchased in different models. Many of the products and services can be purchased directly from the vendors. However, there are also a large number of products only sold through vendor application resellers (VARs). VARs are resellers that will sell you the licenses for many Microsoft and other products. These VARs can provide implementation and hosting services as well in a bundled fashion if needed.

There are thousands of VARS to select from. I recommend finding one that is local and large enough to have resources and other technical experts on their team. VARs can help you analyze different software products to determine right-size applications for you.

As an example, when we were trying to find a general ledger for our firm, Microsoft provided multiple products for us to select from. We leaned heavily on VARs to help us navigate the product shelf and make purchase recommendations. We ultimately hired a partner with implementation and ongoing support as a bundled service.

Services

Managed Services

We've discussed managed services earlier, but let's formally define that as an information technology service provider that operates and assumes responsibility for providing the client a defined set of services. Services would include monitoring, patching, maintenance, security enhancements, and all human capital required to maintain the healthy operation of that service/function. These types of services usually fall into the following categories: network setup and administration, network security, desktop and end-user support, data center setup and management, data backup and recovery, email services, web hosting, and telephony services.

Application Services

Some firms decide to outsource portions of their application portfolio and hire a full-service application team. There are many offshore partners in this space that would have a significant amount of the support offshore and a small footprint of the team onshore to interact with your employees. I do not recommend trying to outsource your applications at the same time that you are moving data centers. However, supplementing your team with extra resources will leverage the knowledge of your in-house team and provide more hands, both to execute this project and to support the production environment in parallel. If any of the application services are outsourced at your parent company, you will need to work with that outsourcing partner and renegotiate the support contract for your new firm. You will be able to continue to operate under the legacy master services agreement for a period of time.

Consulting Services

You will find that for every gap you identified in the services and skills assessment process, there are consultants that you can hire. Typical examples are strategy consultants, management consultants, operations consultants, financial advisory consultants, human resource consultants, and IT consultants. That's a LOT of consultants!

One success factor is to know that you do not have to hire these people as full-time contractors on your project. You can hire them full-time for a short period to help quickly create your vision and strategy to build your team and define your operational model. You can also hire them for short-term consultant gigs to do a specific project that lasts only one or two days, or as in the HR consultant, to help staff with a particularly critical role. Many of them prefer to provide advice and will request a more strategic relationship that has them on a retainer basis. This kind of relationship gives you access to them and their expertise with a certain level of responsiveness and a certain level of engagement, for a monthly fee.

I do recommend that you consider having access to a strategist and an operational consultant in this capacity to participate in your strategy and planning process and to review recommendations from your team and the vendors you hire.

IT Consultants

You can hire technical expertise and independent IT consultants for every domain space in your IT services portfolio. These people are available for one-off project work. Also, many are willing to engage with your firm on a right-to-hire model, which can be ideal by allowing you to make a quick staffing decision and then decide on the appropriate fit of the individual as they start executing the project. I find this approach to staffing open positions great in that it allows you to mobilize very quickly. Sometimes, within just a couple of weeks of identifying a need, you can have people in-house helping you.

The only barrier to bringing them in will be the onboarding processes. Your legacy parent firm may be a bottleneck for you if you are still dependent on them for this function. If you are responsible for onboarding new employees and contractors at this point but do not have defined processes yet, you may also find the hiring process too burdensome. Fortunately, as mentioned above, there are many HR consultants available for hire to assist you with defining the operational onboarding processes for your organization.

Project Management and Project Resources

Just as you can hire for any IT technical domain, you can also staff any other project resource need with consultants. These roles include program management, project management, business analysts, quality assurance testers, software developers, and engineers of any domain of expertise. There are a large number of staffing firms available to help you. There are both large IT consulting firms that will help run the project for you and niche firms that offer specialized skills.

If you'd like help with vendor research or selection, please reach out to me for support and advice. I am available for both consulting assignments in this area and on retainer as an executive coach and advisor. You will find my contact information on the copyright page. If I am not available to support your project based on availability, I can also refer you to others who can help in this area.

Up Next

In the next section, I address the importance of creating a real partnership with your vendor. I even argue that the success of your spin-off effort depends on it!

5.

Create a Culture
of Partnership

Up until now, we have been talking about vendors, and I've purposely interspersed the word "partner" as well. A critical success factor is to create a culture of partnership amongst your teams and those at the vendor(s). This particular value and mindset ended up being one of the most important things that helped my spin-off projects be successful. From day one, I insisted that my team treated the RFP winners as partners rather than just vendors.

"We", *Not* "Us" and "Them"

The contract is with the vendor. The "vendor" is the company or firm that is hired. However, a company is a bunch of people. These people, like your team, want to be treated with respect, they want to add value, feel valued, and they want to be successful. They are individuals. So it only made sense to me that the people who worked at the vendor must be treated as our partners and that they get excited about the success of the project as if they were part of the team. If they could get invested in a successful outcome, they would be just as motivated as the employees to make great things happen.

I realize this probably doesn't work for all types of vendors. For example, a large software company isn't necessarily going to act like a partner when you are only buying 500 copies, and they sell billions of licenses across the globe. However, the biggest vendors in your portfolio that you depend on day in, day out should be treated as partners as much as possible, and not just as hired hands.

Two Partnership Experiences

In both spin-offs I was involved with, I can think of a critical defining moment where this approach was pivotal in the success of the project. In the first spin-off, as CIO of the firm, I hosted a face-to-face kickoff session with both my management team and that of our primary partner, the data center management team. This meeting was entirely funded from the project and included not only management but all senior people from both firms who would be engaged in the effort. The two to three days of planning together solidified the team right away. We shared with them all of the details of the problem that we had on the table, what we were up against in terms of timelines, and how much we needed them for the spin-off to be successful. It was in the spirit of true partnership and transparency. This kickoff session helped set the tone for the entire relationship.

In my second spin-off, as an IT consultant and advisor acting as the interim CTO, I was asked to help recover a project that was falling behind schedule. This same strategy was engaged in building relationships with the management of the infrastructure services firm that had already been selected before my engagement. Early during my involvement, I went to the managed service facility and spent two days with their leadership team face-to-face to make sure that we had agreement on all of the things we were trying to accomplish together. This included operational readiness activities. We brainstormed the issues; we got agreement on definitions; we discussed the terms in the statement of work. We put together an operational model for post-go-live services that had been neglected in the earlier phases of the project. Their appreciation of the progress we made in the two-day collaboration proved to me that real partnership with their people was, in fact, the success factor.

Sometimes these topics are not easy to tackle, but face-to-face time with your partner provides tremendous value that is essential to build trust, respect, collaboration, and partnership. Once you choose your vendor, I can't urge you enough to start that relationship by doing all you can to create a culture of partnership with them. You'll find too that the success of your spin-off depends on it.

Up Next

In the next chapter, I discuss how to start the vendor selection process by securing funding to hire your first few strategic partnerships.

6.

Secure Initial
Funding

If you have just discovered that the sale will occur, it is very likely that only a very small inner circle of individuals is aware that this is happening. Often, the sale of a firm, a strategic review, a capital restructuring, or any other business merger and acquisition type of activity is not announced until there's been a leak. A leak can occur if there's a lot of people who are actually "in the tent." Somewhere, somehow, someone will make a mistake and talk to someone, or slip and imply the sale is happening. Up until that point, there is a fair amount of runway for the senior IT leader to do some initial planning.

Let's look at how you can take advantage of that precious runway time in light of securing some funding so you can hire some key partners.

Your First Moves

It's during this time that I recommend you do a lot of the research on the vendors and partners that you would pursue. This research does not mean calling the partners at this time but thinking about your organization, the domains you need to build, and starting to create the list of firms within each of those domain areas. Educating yourself upfront is very important.

With some education under your belt, it's time to hire a few of the strategists that we discussed earlier. You should start putting together a proposal for your senior leadership team. This proposal is meant to fund the strategists who will help you define your strategic partner strategy, establish the vendors/partners selection criteria, and define types of vendors and consultants available to you—the important issues discussed in this first section of the book. Bringing in this early support will be critical.

The vendor selection process for the more critical and strategic IT services is about a three-month process. It includes identification of requirements, RFP, scoring, legal contracting, and statement of work activity. Depending on how busy the legal team is, it could even take longer.

Also, I recommend you find a program manager or IT consulting firm that can help brainstorm how to execute and estimate the cost and time of your spin-off effort. As we will discuss in the next section of the book, you most likely will not be able to implement this with only your existing team.

Initial Funding

The initial funding is meant for hiring both of these skills, the strategist and the program manager. You want to find a strategist who has experience with implementing the types of IT services you need to build. Ideally, you will find someone that also brings a vendor selection process and scorecard with them (if you don't already have a process defined in-house). Ideally, you'll also hire a program management firm or individual that has executed a spin-off before.

You should add to the funding a request for a second strategist or advisor on retainer on a monthly basis that you can go to for coaching, advice, and a second opinion on all recommendations coming from the others.

SECTION BRIEF

As already discussed, if you are in the early stages of your project, then you probably got the most out of this first section, "Prepare: Planning and Partners." We dedicated this section to considering your overall strategy and your selection of partners to help you along the way. We ended, of course, with this short chapter on securing funding for those first two very important partners, a strategist and program manager.

Keep in mind that I, too, am available to work with you in a supporting role. I know how exciting and high stakes it is to lead a spin-off, and having me at your side guiding you could make all the difference. Don't hesitate to contact me to discuss the possibility of our working together. You will find my contact information on the copyright page.

Up Next

Up next is Section 2, called "People." In it, we consider your team, the people you've been working with for years, and those who you'll be working with on the spin-off project and beyond, in the new standalone organization. Section 2 provides you with tools to lead your people to success, especially as you are all chartering into unfamiliar waters together.

PEOPLE

7.

Define the Organizational Structure

As we begin Section 2 "People," we want to start by defining your organizational structure to support all the IT services you will be responsible for delivering to your business and its customers. If you have been running as a complete standalone division with almost full autonomy, this might be a quick task. However, it's very probable that some of the IT services are delivered outside of your group.

This first step in defining your organizational structure is critical, and there are hundreds of ways to structure your organization. In this chapter, I give my thoughts on the different departments and teams that you might want to build out.

Corporate/Enterprise Services

Some organizations lump this group of corporate/enterprise services into the space of "application support." For our purposes, they get their own section. We will define this as the financial applications: procurement, general ledger; human resource applications: HRMS system, payroll, benefits management, recruiting, training platforms, employee collaboration tools (corporate intranet and employee chat);

and legal applications: archiving, email/text/chat surveillance and discovery tools, and contract management repositories.

You can see this is a broad group. The amount of business relationship management, prioritization, and operational oversight of these functions can require the full-time attention of one of your senior leaders.

Infrastructure Services

I generally lump into this group the data center, network management, service desk, desktop support, telephony, and employee productivity software support. It's likely that if your team was just application development and support at the legacy firm, the senior leader of this group is one of the most critical hires you have ahead of you. Depending on the size of your organization, this is often a CTO position reporting to you, the CIO. If your title is CTO, then this is likely a senior vice president. Ideally, you will name or recruit for this position early in your process, so they can be part of the vendor selection processes if a third party will support any of the services.

Each of the functions as described below, may or may not need a separate leader. This decision will depend on the size of your organization and the skills of the people you have on your team.

As a note, I have also seen situations where the infrastructure organization is large, so the CIO has decided to break this into two groups, with one being data center, network, and telephony, and the second being service desk, desktop support, employee productivity software, and security fulfillment. Your exact structure will vary, but you will need a solution for all of these services.

Data Center Management, Network Management, Telephony

This group manages the maintenance (upgrades, enhancements, and patching) and operations (monitoring, backup, and restoration of service) of the data center, MPLS, external internet service, telephony services, and all the equipment located within the primary facility, its backup location, and all physical equipment and facilities in each of your physical locations. Included in this function is managing any vendors that you have contracted to participate in the delivery of these services.

Service Desk, Desktop Support, Employee Productivity Software Support

The functions in this group include managing the internal- and external-facing help desk functions, phone queues, the assignment of all help tickets, and the staff, both internal and the vendors hired to support these services. This set of functions includes defining the standard desktop/laptop builds, the patching and upgrading processes, the purchasing/leasing of employee hardware, the managing and administration of employee productivity applications, and the distribution of software that will run on employee machines. License and inventory management are critical activities of the group as well.

You will want to consider the maintenance and operations of the file servers, network printers, and localized storage and backup capabilities with this group although the network services team can easily manage them. The skills on your team or how you purchase these capabilities from vendors will help you determine where these should be aligned in your group.

There is a unique set of service desk delivery applications and software that are running in an organization, not only in IT but also in the business units if the business supports customers directly. Included in these applications are queue management tools, ticketing systems, and client relationship management applications. These applications would typically fall under the management of the service desk manager as well for both maintenance and operations. These functions can be under a single leader or run as multiple departments.

In addition to managing the above functions related to the service desk, I have often seen the service desk manager in charge of change management, incident management, and security fulfillment functions that are described in the Production Readiness section (section 4) of this book.

Application Support Management

If you are genuinely in a spin-off from a large firm, this is often the most substantial part of your portfolio of services that your existing team is providing. That would lead me to believe that you have a good idea on how to structure this group. There are as many ways to structure the application portfolio as there are functions. I offer this advice, if nothing else: split the portfolio into at least two groups, the internal or back-office applications (used by the business units of the firm) and client/customer applications. The reason for this split is that the SLAs and business requirements for incident recovery times are likely to be different and drive different demands on your teams.

Marketing and Communication

The chief marketing officer (CMO) position has become a more technical role in organizations as more of a firm's marketing takes place in the digital space. Often the CMO, in partnership with the

CIO, has a critical role in driving innovation for a firm. As the CIO is often dealing with many internal issues, I've noticed we can become bogged down in the weeds of delivery and risk that innovation becomes more and more driven by the business units.

To stop this trend, the CIO will need to have a great team managing the day-to-day services of all the other functions. This way, the CIO can invest a significant amount of their time with the marketing and communication group, and the CMO in particular. A marketing and communications unit that is leading-edge in using cloud-based technologies, though, may be reluctant to partner with you as you bring process, policy, and structure to their teams. You may be perceived as slowing them down.

Regardless of how you integrate, they have a portfolio of applications that do need to be supported: external-facing websites, content management systems, client relationship management systems, advertising and campaign management tools, social media management, webinar and collaboration tools, many business intelligence and data analytic systems, and lead management products. Be aware there are many third-party vendors in this space getting the attention of the CMO and working directly with them without your involvement.

Security—Governance, Policy, Operations, Incidents

The chief security officer of a firm is another critical role to fill right away. This role can report into IT, compliance, or even to the CEO directly. If the function does fall into the IT organization as it has in my experience, you can move some of the security fulfillment and operational tasks from the service desk to this senior leader. However, most of the candidates I've seen and talked to for this position all wanted to stay high-level, set policy, and be involved only with advice and governance. As you break away from the parent firm, you need to establish the policies quickly, especially if you need to have HIPPA or SOX compliance. The security needs of a firm are niche, based on different industries. My recommendation is to hire this role right away or hire a consultant to fill this position immediately until you can find the right full-time candidate.

Project Management Office

Your spin-off effort can't run on the expertise of your senior management team alone. You need a team of project managers. You may already have some that are coming with you from the parent company.

As you spin-off and create the standalone organization, I suggest that this is an independent group with a senior leader reporting to you. I have worked in several organizations where this function was in the business unit reporting to a head of strategy, rather than reporting to the CIO. I always found this a difficult alignment. My experience and preference are that this should be an IT function. I have only worked with one CIO who felt completely different. Their opinion was that if it was a business function, IT wouldn't be responsible when things were not executing correctly. Whichever way you prefer, I recommend that you centralize the function and get all the project leaders into a single organization.

Data Management, Analytics, Business Intelligence

In today's world, there are more data analytics and business intelligence initiatives than ever. In addition to the traditional database maintenance and operations that include data backups and storage management, I've added business intelligence. We've seen the importance of data to an organization's rise to the C-suite. Here's Wikipedia's definition of the newly emerging chief data officer (CDO):

> A **chief data officer** (CDO) is a corporate **officer** responsible for enterprise-wide governance and utilization of information as an asset, via **data** processing, analysis, **data** mining, information trading and other means. CDOs report mainly to the **chief** executive **officer** (CEO).

I think it's great to see this position getting the attention it deserves. However, if you are a smaller firm, this position likely will be a senior executive already in the organization, possibly the CMO, the head of recruiting/sales, or even the chief financial officer. It might also be someone who is named the CDO and reports into one of these positions. Either way, you still need to worry about the pipes, the raw data itself, and the applications that run on all that data. That includes supporting all the business apps, reporting needs, data warehousing tools, business intelligence, and trending tools, etc.

Sample Functional Org Chart

This chart tries to suggest a structure that you can use as a starting point. I recommend a head of applications for the different groups to report in to. I've also made the security fulfillment team a slightly different shade to call out that this group can just as easily report into the information security office.

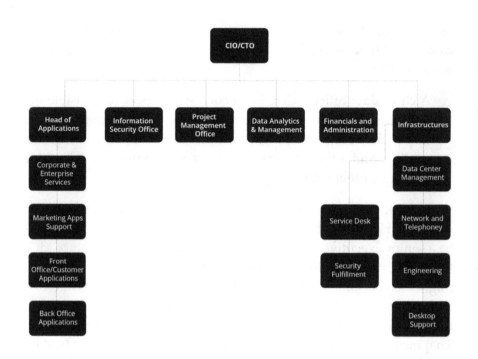

Up Next

With this chapter's definition of the possible functions in your organization, in the next chapter, we'll explore your team and how to determine if they have the skillsets required to execute a successful spin-off and run IT operations as a standalone company.

8.

Assess for the
Critical Skills

There are many factors to consider when determining if your team has the right skillsets required both to execute a successful separation program and to run IT operations as a standalone company. The largest influence will depend on the level of autonomy the department had in the larger organization you are spun off from.

Now that you have defined the functions in your organization, you can start interviewing your people to see if anyone has skills in these areas and if there is interest amongst existing team members in those opportunities. One of my mistakes is that I didn't give my internal people enough opportunity to apply for positions because I was moving too fast. Later, I learned that some people wanted a chance at the positions. The takeaway: don't make this same mistake!

Cultural Fit

I did give a few people on my team opportunities to shift from the roles that they had to very different positions in the new firm because their old roles were no longer needed and they had been good loyal employees for us. Unfortunately, not all of these people were successful in their new roles. Several of them either had to be let go or decided to leave on their own because the culture and pace of a small firm were just too different from navigating and working in a large company. Seeing these dedicated people fail in their new roles was difficult, because I had always prided myself on a management style that focused on coaching and growing the people around me. I admit I was slow to make the decision that they weren't succeeding.

You need to be ready for this reality: not everybody will make it through your separation program. The skills that are needed to be successful in a large organization are not the same as what's needed in a dynamic smaller firm. Your people need to be flexible and nimble. They need to be excellent communicators and capable of raising issues early. The team needs to be comfortable working in an environment where policy and procedures are not yet defined.

In the spin-offs I led, the need for defined processes was a contributing factor to people leaving. A few of the best and most dedicated managers in the large organization, who were experts at navigating the policies and procedures of the legacy firm, were lost in the new world of the spin-off where nothing was defined. It might make sense to have these people assigned to define your operational processes and to do this early in the project. This shift may help them succeed in the transition to the new world.

Technical Competency and Maturity

After the first assessment, you'll need to make a second pass and ask yourself an even more difficult question: "Does each individual have the technical competency and maturity to be successful in the new company?" Although it sounds harsh to think this way, you can't have all average people in your organization. You need to make sure that, if complacency has set in on any of them, you recognize that the bar must be raised in the smaller firm. It is difficult for mediocre performers to survive in the new world. It is better to take an honest look at performance upfront and make changes quickly.

In addition to looking at performance, there can be a need to "right-staff" a team and restructure how a team is composed. For example, if you have programmers, notice if they are all junior or mid-level programmers, and determine if there are no senior leaders or architects on the team. For example, you might need to replace a team of one mid-level and four junior programmers with one lead, two mid-levels, and two junior programmers. Fortunately, you can use this opportunity to help with eliminating the marginal performers.

This assessment is true for your senior leadership team as well. You will likely need to give them a chance in the new world unless their function is being eliminated in your new organizational model. Be prepared to have in place thirty-, sixty-, and ninety-day goals for people moved into positions that might be stretch assignments. Be willing to admit if they are not going to be the right fit.

Program Management

Often, project and program management are centralized in another area of the firm, and these resources are not identified as being part of the sold entity. If there are project management resources that have been closely aligned with your business unit, you should anticipate needing to make a case that they should come with the sale. In other times, your particular application group has been running very independently and perhaps you're far-flung and located somewhere other than the parent. In this case, you may have the project management skills on staff already, and they are tagged as resources included in the sale.

In either case, it's important to know that not all project managers are capable of running this kind of program. There are components that are extremely technical. The definition of a program I am using is a collection of different projects happening concurrently that are required to be delivered in a particular order for the larger project to be successful. The program manager provides a level of oversight and structure for the series of underlying smaller projects.

There are many projects, and dealing with a list of more than a dozen projects can get overwhelming. Our programs were managed more effectively by bundling the projects into groups that we called workstreams. To be a great program manager requires that an individual become a common thread across all of the workstreams. You'll need somebody who can facilitate and manage issue escalations, orchestrate issue resolution brainstorming discussions, and drive activities and dependencies across projects within a workstream and across the workstreams themselves. This individual is like a project manager on steroids: they're a super multitasker, very organized, and willing to go the extra mile and work a lot of extra hours. They are great communicators, they're creative, and they are excellent at providing transparency.

This program management skill may not be a person on your staff but be your role by default. On my first effort, this was the strength that I brought to the table. I had run large programs in the past, and it felt natural for me to run the IT department like a program; day-to-day production was just another workstream. I didn't have time to manage the program administrative details, and I don't think you should try to do this either. Hire a program manager who has most of the skills mentioned above. Also, ready yourself as the one who might need to be the glue across all the components to pull this thing off successfully.

Finding all these skills in a single person is very difficult. It necessitates the creation of the right program governance for the projects. They will require steering committees with consistent members across. Ideally, these steering committee members will have had program management as a background. In some organizations, the project management resources are in the business organization and not in IT. I highly recommend that you don't rely on a business program manager to run the whole project and that you hire a program manager who will report directly to you for the duration of the effort. Without this critical role, you won't have as much insight and transparency into the program as you'll need.

Vendor Management

The next critical skill to discuss is vendor management. Vendor management is a complex set of skills that cover a broad set of activities that include contract negotiation, production incident management, change management, and vendor selection. There's a whole life cycle related to vendor management, and it likely requires some new skills for the management team in your organization, especially if you are a small division coming from a large corporation. Sometimes this particular skill is centralized in the procurement department.

If you're small enough that all your managers have some expertise in managing vendors, that is great! In either case, new operational procedures will be needed. I recommend starting from standard operating procedures that exist. If there aren't any, you can leverage the information available on the internet or from an operational consultant who has managed to establish them before. Starting this activity early in the project is important. Establishing them before looking for vendors would position you to include them as part of the vendor selection process. You will be caught off-guard and possibly come up with delays if operational readiness isn't tackled early enough.

A Final Thought

On the second spin-off I was involved with, I went to work with a few of the executives whom I had worked with before. After about thirty days on the project, I met with the CEO of the firm who asked my honest opinion on the talent of the senior team. The project had struggled a bit, so it was a fair question: "Do we have the right people on our senior team?"

My feedback to the CEO, and now to you:

Not everyone who is good at building things is also good at running things, and the opposite is true as well.

To be successful at both the separation project and operational support, you need both kinds of people.

People fall into these two categories; you need the balance of both on your team.

In my opinion, it's not usual that the people who are the builders and the entrepreneurs come from the middle management of a large firm. You need to supplement the senior team and recruit a few outsiders for the new management functions. The current team are most likely experts at running things that are already in place.

Let me repeat: I would be happy to work with you in your spin-off effort. I am passionate about coaching and collaborating, and I'm also experienced at leading spin-offs. Contact me so we can discuss how I could work with you. You will find my contact information on the copyright page.

Up Next

In the next chapter, we discuss taking your list of hires and open positions that you need to build out your team and then doing it: building out your team.

9.

Build the Team

At this point, you've determined what the target organization will look like and soon you will define the execution of the separation project into a series of projects. You have taken a good look at both yourself, your team, and the skills that you all bring to the new organization. You are ready to start formalizing the list of hires and open positions that you need to build out your team.

The first time I pulled together the list of hires and open positions, I was looking at close to forty people that we needed to add to the team. That's a lot of hiring! If your list is even half this long, you'll need a staffing strategy.

Leverage Your Management Team

This step—building your team—isn't possible unless it is now public information that you have been sold or are being sold. Now more than ever, it is important to leverage your full set of leaders to staff the organization. The first step is to identify *all* the leaders, not just your senior team, who are impacted by the new organization model. You should walk them through your vision of the organization and your thought process for establishing this structure. If you have decided to make staffing moves and shift people's responsibilities, you should talk to those individuals ahead of time and *then* share the changes more broadly. It is imperative that you engage in transparent communication from the start. Transparency is the key to getting buy-in from your people.

Until the new leaders have been hired into the organization, temporarily assign your list of hires and open positions to the leaders of the departments that are responsible for the given function or to the leaders identified with building the teams. If possible, always staff the open management positions first. Hiring management first allows the incoming leaders to staff their departments and perhaps leverage their network of contacts to bring in talent that they have worked with before. This strategy works particularly well for the new IT functions being built out.

Use Trusted Staffing Partners

You might have a list of recruiters, staffing firms, and temp agencies that you have worked with already, or you might not. It will depend on the size of your organization and the types of activities and projects that you have run in the past. If you have a list of approved partners from the legacy parent, this is a great place to start. You need to determine whether you can work with them under the contract provisions of the parent under a transition services agreement (TSA). Of course, this will bind you to the agreements and conversion costs, etc., that are already in place, but you should be able to get resumes quickly.

If you have not used staffing agencies in the past, or your TSA does not account for this ability, it's easy to pull together a list of local and national firms that can help you fill tech positions. The barrier to speed to market, in this case, will be how quickly your legal team can create a master services agreement with the new firms.

Your new company's human resource officer (HRO), if one has been identified, may already have identified partners they'd like you to work with. It's best to let them know what your hiring/staffing plan looks like and with them, vet the list of firms you want to work with. Also, meet with the firm's general counsel and legal team to determine if contracts are best used under the TSA or as the new standalone company. At a minimum, they need to know which firms to put on a list of contracting work that they will need to complete on their own project plan.

Identify Need for Recruiters

As you review the list of roles you need to add to the team, there will be a few positions that you know must be permanent and are critical to the organization. If those are senior positions, you should consider using either a local or national recruiting firm. There are different placement fees, but if you use a national firm and are willing to support relocation fees, you will obviously find the pool of candidates is much broader. If you are in a local market where there is access to many tech leaders, a local firm may be enough and will keep the costs lower. As a rule of thumb, using any of these recruiting firms entails a finder's fee, which is a percentage of the new hire's salary or total compensation.

Other full-time positions are more easily filled by using online job boards and posting positions to these and by announcing or advertising them on LinkedIn. This may be enough to find candidates. Remember to talk with the HRO for their thoughts on the best approach, so that they are aware of all avenues being pursued.

All temporary roles can be filled with consultants, consulting firms, and individual staffing agencies as mentioned earlier. In my spin-off experiences, we used staffing agencies to find candidates on a "right-to-hire" contract. The conversion costs vary by firm depending on the MSA you have in place. Often your legal team will negotiate a term by which if the individual remains as a contractor for a period of time, there will not be a conversion fee at all.

Vet Candidates Effectively

The amount of time needed to review resumes, screen candidates with phone interviews, schedule face-to-face meetings, and orchestrate the decision-making process for each position cannot be underestimated. This is time-consuming and a heavy lift for everyone in the organization involved. It is best if you can standardize processes to streamline things. I recommend for each position that you and the team identify the decision-maker and the people whose opinions are critical to the process. Define the critical skills you want in each position.

For the face-to-face meetings, determine an order of interviewing so that if any person on the interview team says no emphatically about a candidate during the process, then that candidate is let go early rather than wasting the time of your other team members who would have to interview them later in the cycle. This approach does require a little orchestration upfront and a dedicated interview room where the candidate stays while the interviewers rotate in and out of the room. This is a process that I experienced years ago when interviewing at a large West Coast software company, and it was very effective. I've used this process for the last fourteen years as a result!

Centralize the Onboarding

Finding and recruiting great talent is only the beginning. You need to shuffle everyone through an onboarding process that does background checks, follows up on references, identifies the physical location of where they will work once onsite, acquires the equipment they'll use, and gets them access to all the required systems and tools needed to complete their work. In addition, finance and procurement systems all need to be set up appropriately to handle the review and payment of invoices for all these contractors.

During the first few weeks and months after the initial announcement, you will be operating under the TSA, and the legacy parent will be doing most of the onboarding work. You might find they don't have the capacity to resource all of those new hires as quickly as you would like. Typical lead times for bringing someone into the organization start to take longer. Plan for that! You might lose great candidates if they can't start within two weeks.

A critical goal will be to centralize all of the onboarding processes through a single person on your team. Doing this can help you anticipate costs and keep you aware of when people are starting. You'll need to track the details on what hardware and equipment are being handed out. Consequently, although I am talking about moving quickly, you do need to be structured, focused, and organized.

Up Next

With your team built, or even while it's getting built, you cannot forget everyone's morale. For the separation to go well and for the spin-off to be a success, you must keep in mind the importance of motivating and inspiring your leadership of the organization. In the next chapter, I give you some advice about this.

10.

Lead, Motivate, Inspire

Have you heard that old piece of advice: "Hire the right people and get out of their way"? My guess is that advice is coming from people who have experience at leading when everything is already set up, running, and working like a well-oiled machine. I've seen that advice work successfully in a fully operational and mature company.

Currently, you are running a spin-off and a separation program. Yes, of course, you need to hire the right people. However, you are running a program with a ton of moving parts—parallel workstreams and concurrent activities—and everything has to come together and coalesce at the same time to go live with the separation. This effort requires a different strategy than "getting out of the way"!

In this chapter, I outline the best practices of my spin-off experiences, so you can create a strategy that will work well for you and your spin-off.

Create a Compelling Vision

I can't claim to have the perfect answer for every situation because every situation requires a different type of leadership. The strategy I've found that worked for my efforts was to first start with a compelling vision.

Many of your employees are going to be afraid of what the new organization will be like, and most will feel like their future is uncertain. To create a calming force for your organization, you must create a compelling future vision of what it will be like when you are the standalone company. You need to embody a level of energy and excitement that is infectious. Establish key messages about how exciting it will be when you all are the leaders of your own organization, creating your own policies, and establishing your own processes and procedures. Frame it as everyone's chance to finally implement all the lessons learned from your collective years of experience at how things can improve! You and your team are going to create an environment where all of you are in charge of your own destiny!

It will help if you do believe this. It is such an exciting time. Building a standalone company and having an opportunity to lead the organization through the effort is a once-in-a-lifetime experience. You need to rise to the calling! If you haven't yet caught the independence fever, get an executive coach to work with and get excited. Your energy around this will be apparent to everyone.

I can help you get excited! Again, you will find my contact information on the copyright page.

Share the Vision with Everyone!

Technology people hate meetings. They hate getting out from their desks and going to meetings in person. A lot of them think it's a waste of time and takes them away from their assignments. There are a few outliers, but this is the consistent culture I've seen at every company I have ever worked for.

To effectively lead, inspire, and motivate, you will need to spend a lot of time in front of the entire organization, with mandatory meetings. Yes, mandatory and face-to-face, if possible. If they are not mandatory, people won't come, and they won't hear your message. You need everyone on the same page.

I held these types of meetings every week. Sometimes the mandatory meetings were ad-hoc with only a two-hour notice. Don't be afraid to do this if something significant is going on that you need to communicate. In the initial meeting, talk openly to the organization about its structure and the number of positions you need to add. Talk about how there is a significant drain when adding so many people to an organization. It's possible that you will be adding as much as fifty percent growth to the team for almost a year. That level of growth and then the subsequent contraction that occurs at the end of the project is a lot of change. Get in front of your team, talk with them every step of the way, and openly empathize about the drain it takes when bringing on new teammates. This is critical.

Your level of honesty and transparency is so important to getting the organization bought into the vision. I've already mentioned that many of them will be having anxiety. They are sitting there waiting to see. To see what the culture is, what you will do, and how this change is going to impact them. The quicker you can give them a vision of what the future is like, instead of letting them create their own visions in their heads, the faster everyone will be working towards that shared vision that you've created. I recommend that you include everyone in the organization in these sessions, whether they are an employee, contractor, or service provider. Everyone needs to see where the team is heading and how they fit into that future state.

Educate About How You Will Execute

As you get everyone acquainted with your vision of the future state of the organization, also educate them on the program and the separation plan needed to get there. If you have already identified the leaders of each of the workstreams, then introduce them and let them give updates and share the strategy, key deliverables, timelines, risks, and even issues, in the spirit of ultimate transparency.

I recommend sharing information about the total budget, strategic drivers, and success factors. There might be a reaction here because you do have your partners in the room if you are following my advice about including everyone. I have received feedback at times that you shouldn't share information about the budget with your partners, but I feel this is important to make everyone feel part of the team. They want to be successful too. Giving them transparency is the best way to get everyone vested in the outcome.

You might be a little worried about over-sharing. Obviously, don't share confidential information, but by showing your people that you trust them, they end up both **motivated** and **inspired**.

Express Vulnerabilities

If we build on this thought of creating trust and inspiring the team, then I want to suggest that you share more than transparency on your vision, the strategy, and your thought process on why you want things done in a certain way. You should consider expressing your insecurities and vulnerabilities. Are there parts of the effort that you are more worried about than others? Why are you concerned?

Ask the team in a collaborative nature for ideas. Let them know that you understand that bringing up ideas in such a large group can be intimidating. Ask them to send you an email or come by your office if they are not comfortable speaking up in a large group. You are not expressing a weakness if you share your concerns with everyone. You are being human in front of your team, and this builds a strong following.

The Power of Focus

The concept of weekly mandatory meetings is for one purpose only: to consistently **reinforce and repeat** the strategy, vision, and execution plan. You need to keep everyone focused on where you are going and remind them of the timelines, risks, issues, etc.

There are three critical leadership books that have had an influence on me that reinforce this message. The first is *Think and Grow Rich* by Napoleon Hill. This book is about much more than getting rich. It is the result of Napoleon Hill interviewing hundreds of the most successful businessmen of the early 20th century over a twenty-year period. From this work, he summarized his findings into a set of principles. You may or may not agree with all of them, but the one message that stuck with me through the years is the power of your mind. You need the desire to succeed, a vision of where you are going, a belief that you will get there, and positive self-talk to convince and motivate yourself when you have moments of doubt. You need a strategy and a plan of how to get there, and you need persistence, constant focus, and the ability to overcome fear or negative beliefs.

The second book is *Unlimited Power* by Tony Robbins. The message that stuck with me from Tony is that you have to have a vision or a goal in mind. You need to know where you are going. Second, you need a plan. Then you just start taking massive action and see if you are getting the results you want. If yes, great; if not, course correct and try something else. His advice on fast-tracking is to get a model and coach, someone who has done this before, so you can learn from their mistakes.

The more recent book is *The Secret* by Rhonda Byrne, which is based on the law of attraction. Its overall message is that what you think and feel is what you attract to yourself in your life. Think and believe you can do it, and you will manifest what you are trying to accomplish.

I personally use these approaches to be driven and to lead others. My success strategy calls me to use these same principles to lead organizations and to keep large groups of people consistently focusing their attention on and rallied around the common goal.

Celebrate the Wins!

Okay, I know this is the same advice as in all the other leadership books, so let this be a reminder. Celebrate successes publicly in front of everyone, praise people when they do an excellent job and when they bring up questions or have the courage to ask questions in front of the group. Have parties, buy ice cream, thank them, appreciate the team, and tell them they are awesome.

Celebrate the lessons! This one is more difficult, but if things don't go well, share that with them too. You want everyone to learn and move on to the next win!

Don't just celebrate the end. Celebrate all the little steps along the way. This is a marathon. Everyone on the team needs the encouragement. Everyone needs to feel the progress.

Watch-Outs

The biggest advice is to watch out for the potential of leaders on your team who start to behave as "nervous nellies." They will undermine the confidence and progress of the group, but not intentionally. This is the person who always comments, "We can't do it," "It won't work," or "It will take too long." They want to be onboard and successful, but they bring a negative perspective to everything. You won't need to get rid of them necessarily, but you will need to stay sharp and make sure your positive messages are getting out from every direction.

You need to create a culture of "What will it Take?", "What if it were possible?", and "What could we do?" Create an environment where "There is always a way"!

Up Next

I am including a website for the book where I intend to provide bonus videos of some of this information in video format. My intention is to develop this bonus content over time so keep checking back for the most recent additions.

www.howtoleadacorporatespinoff.com/bonuses

The next chapter continues this discussion about culture at the organization. We'll look at it in terms of the new leadership team at the organization and how as leaders you are integral in setting a can-do mindset.

11.

Create a Culture
of Empowerment

The empowering questions at the end of the last chapter are another important lesson from Tony Robbins. Let's look at them again:

You need to create a culture of "What will it take?", "What if it were possible?", "What could we do?" Create an environment where "There is always a way"!

If anyone comes to you and says, "I don't know what to do, it can't be done." You can respond with an empowering question, such as, "If we knew what to do, what might be our first step?"

What Is Empowerment?

In the spin-offs I led, with this spirit of "What will it take?" I asked myself all these same questions as I looked both at the team and the new leaders. The culture I tried to create was one of empowerment.

I ask you to consider if this might be the right approach for your team as well. The definition of empowerment, according to Wikipedia, is:

The term **empowerment** refers to measures designed to increase the degree of autonomy and self-determination in people and in communities in order to enable them to represent their interests in a responsible and self-determined way, acting on their own authority. It is the process of becoming stronger and more confident, especially in controlling one's life and claiming one's rights.

My definition of empowerment is an organization of leaders that believe, "We are independent, creative, and filled with possibilities. We will always find a way. Anything is possible, and we can make it work. Failure is not an option. There is always a way."

What Is Culture?

To have a group of leaders, many of whom were previously middle management in a large firm, embody this level of autonomy and self-determination is going to take a culture shift. In a large firm, middle management is tasked with following rules, processes, and policy set by someone else. To lead a standalone organization to a successful spin-off requires a different mindset, and thus a different culture.

The definition of culture from Wikipedia: "**Culture** is the social behavior and norms found in human societies."

My definition of culture developed from years of reading personal development and leadership books, and from my organizational behavior class I had while completing my master's degree in management. Here is my definition of culture: "a group of people with a common set of attitudes, standards, behaviors, and values."

I've learned that with responsibility comes empowerment. To help your leaders step into their roles and to overcome the patterns established in the old firm, you need to create this new culture and train your leaders on the common set of attitudes, standards, and behaviors that you expect. You need to establish a shared set of values as quickly as possible and get the leaders aligned and feeling responsible for rolling those values out to the organization.

Establish Your Set of Attitudes, Standards, Behaviors, and Values

This step and advice might seem like one of the most challenging tasks ahead of you because it takes more self-assessment and reflection. You must consciously think through what your set of attitudes are, and be clear on your standards, acceptable behaviors, and values. Once established, how to roll them out and make them norms of the leaders on your team can seem like climbing a mountain at the same time as trying to execute this project!

The best way to establish the values and behaviors is to find or resurface business and leadership books that you or others recommend that have shaped your style and approach. If you haven't found many that resonate with you, don't worry. I am going to share my eight secret weapons. These books and concepts have influenced me throughout most of my career, and in my spin-off efforts, I called on all of them to create the right culture for my successful teams. I will summarize the lesson or impact these have had on my groups, so you can evaluate if they might work for you.

1—*The One Minute Manager*

The One Minute Manager by Kenneth Blanchard and Spencer Johnson was first published in 1982 and is now considered a classic. In 1988, when I took a semester off from college to work as a programmer, I was introduced to this book as part of a formal corporate training program at the Travelers Insurance Company.

The principal concepts of this book are the three techniques of an effective manager : one-minute goals, one-minute praisings, and one-minute reprimands. This simple structure set the tone for my entire communication style, which has always been very direct and to the point.

I worked with people to set objectives. When things went great, I was the first to praise them, and when things went wrong, I often redirected—quickly and unfortunately curtly at times too. This didn't always make me liked, but the feedback I received is that people knew what I was thinking and where they stood with me. In turn, this made me predictable and transparent to them, which they appreciated. More than anything, I wanted transparency in the organizations I led because it was always important to me as a member of a team to understand whether I was on task and supporting the overall objectives. I wanted to know if there was alignment or if I needed to change course. Because I personally wanted feedback from my managers, I always aspired to provide feedback for others when in a leadership role myself. *The One Minute Manager* is what instilled in me, early in my career, an awareness of the need for and value of frequent feedback.

2—Forming–Storming–Norming–Performing Model of Group Development

The forming–storming–norming–performing model of group development was first proposed by Bruce Tuckman in 1965. I first learned this model at Rensselaer Polytechnic Institute's executive master's program in 2002. Six of us were working in a team throughout the entire program, and organizational development class was one of our first two courses.

The first concept we learned was group dynamics. To become a highly functioning team, all groups would go through four stages. Learning this concept while actively struggling with the storming phase of my new group made this a permanent part of my leadership repertoire forever afterward.

There is a lot of information about this topic on the internet, and I'll add a video of myself presenting this material as one of the bonus items for this book, so look for the links at the end of this chapter. However, let me briefly describe the concept here as I have come to witness and understand it.

All teams come together as a starting point. They are **formed**. At this initial stage, the team or group is given a task or objective, and the people are generally excited and have a high amount of energy. The team comes together and begins to discuss how to approach the objectives, and things slowly start to unravel from there.

Storming starts to occur. Storming is when people begin to argue. Different approaches on how to start, execute, and decide assignments all create a bit of chaos. There are sometimes unclear roles, people are unsure of what they should do, and morale goes down quickly.

Norming is the stage when finally, some acceptable behaviors and modus operandi emerge. Someone is either named the leader or a natural leader rises into the position. The processes and roles become clearer and defined as the team establish a game plan.

Performing is the maturing of the team into a productive and successful group that is able to find solutions and pick up work from each other. Roles are again less clear or important as people cover for each. The team is resolving issues easily and working with a very cooperative spirit. Overall things start to flow.

I don't think you need to spend a lot of time learning this concept. In fact, this simple explanation is probably enough. Knowing that all teams go through these stages of development, and it's a proven fact, will make you a better leader. The interesting thing is that every time a new team member is added to a group that is already performing, they must and will go back to the forming stage. It is likely that the storming process will be much quicker if only one new person is added to an already high performing group, but all stages start again.

I share this with you because you are about to add a significant number of new people to your team and many will be there only temporarily. However, you need to share these stages of group development with your leaders and regularly remind everyone of them because it's important to establish a good process for bringing new people into an existing project. As a result, your leaders can get up to speed quickly and get the teams performing again.

3—The GROW Model

I hope that you were lucky enough to work for an organization that had a formal training program and provided leadership training. I've noticed that only a few firms actually put employee growth and training as a top priority. I was fortunate enough to attend a manager of managers training class in 2007 while working at ING. We got this training not in the US but in the Netherlands. Several things have stuck with me from this one-week full-immersion style of training, but the concept that I carried forward to create a new culture in my organizations is the GROW model derived from Sir John Whitmore's book *Coaching for Performance: The Principles and Practice of Coaching and Leadership*.

This model is an approach to developing your people as a coach, encouraging them to resolve their own issues, rather than solving their problems for them and telling them what to do. My 2007 training class brought in young professionals recently graduated from university for us to practice the model with. After a few attempts and practice, I saw the excitement and empowerment on the faces of my volunteer coachees. It was this experience that helped me see the power of assisting others and leading them to a solution rather than managing them.

Below are the four steps of the GROW model for guiding your employees to be empowered to own and resolve their own issues rather than being told what to do and how to do it by you.

G = Goal First you must establish with your employee-coachee their goal. Ask them, "What are you trying to achieve? What is your ultimate objective?" It may take a few minutes of you posing this question and repeating to them what you are hearing. Often times the person initially expresses the challenge ahead of them rather than the ultimate intention (i.e., goal) of what they are trying to achieve. Your job as the coach is to assist them in framing the goal.

R = Reality Next you guide them to name the challenges and the reality of the situation. You can pose these questions: "Are there limits in resources? Are there constraints? Are there people you are dependent on to achieve your goal?" A few minutes of questioning them and allowing them to explore the situation is required. Make sure this doesn't turn into a venting session. Help them frame the facts, not all the emotion.

O = Options Give your employee some space to work through the facts and reality of their situation, but try to move them quickly into options on how to solve the problem and reach their goal. Try and avoid giving them the option you think will solve their problem quickly. You are a coach in this moment, not solving the problem for them. I like the advice I got from Tony Robbins; for a person to have options, there need to be three different courses of action. If there are only two choices, it's an ultimatum. So, get the person to come up with at least three options.

There is a cheat to get your option on the table. You can ask, "Is there anything preventing you from perhaps trying x?" Sometimes your expertise is needed to provide options. You'll need to be creative here. The idea is to get their ownership of the options.

W = "What will you do?" With the options on the table, get them to discuss the pros and cons of the options. Let them come up with these themselves. If they are at a loss, help them see the strengths and weaknesses of each approach. If you do this, try and remain objective. You are not trying to convince them to do it your way. There are always multiple ways to solve any issue. The critical part of this step is, in the end, to let them choose their option. You don't want them to fail, but if they have a path, even if it's not what you would do, give them the support they need. You are acting as the coach, not the manager.

4—The Sales Leaders Playbook

In 2011, I found Nathan Jamail's book *The Sales Leaders Playbook: Stop Managing, Start Coaching* at the airport on a trip to the Midwest to visit some employees in a remote location. At this point, our spin-off project was complete, but we were still growing as an organization, so it was a fortuitous find!

You might be asking, "Really, Leda? A book for sales leaders?" Yes! This book isn't about how to close a deal. This book is about the fundamentals of how to lead, inspire, and motivate a team. It is important for people who are recently promoted into leadership roles, but it is a great reminder for seasoned leaders as well. It's about team morale, communication, and setting values. This book shows how creating a vision, culture, and common beliefs create high performing teams.

5—The One Minute Manager Meets the Monkey

The One Minute Manager Meets the Monkey by Kenneth Blanchard, William Oncken, Jr, and Hal Burrows is a simple story and helpful approach to prepare your leaders to not take on the work of the people on their teams. It teaches delegation and provides a great way for you and your leaders to create space for yourselves to do your own work and not take on the issues of the rest of the team.

The general principle is that when an employee comes to you with an issue, it's easy to say, "I'll look into it." When you do this, you now own the next task. The employee has basically taken a monkey off of their back and given it to you. I think this message is a reinforcement of the need to use the GROW model. Both are reminders that to empower your employees (and yourself!), you must ask them, "What are you going to do next?"

6—*Start With Why*

I read Simon Sinek's *Start With Why* after seeing Simon Sinek present at a conference I attended in 2011. Here are Simon's key points of the book as summarized in this five-minute Youtube video by Simon himself: **https://www.youtube.com/watch?v=IPYeCltXpxw**

He talks of the golden circle, which is really three concentric circles (i.e., in a bullseye format) with the center of the bullseye being "why." The second inner circle is "what," and the third outer circle is "how."

I love this simple structure because it is a great reminder that you can inspire others only if you get them rallied around the "why." If they can get on board with why you are doing the project or why you are asking them to do something, then they can line up around your "what" and "how."

The message for you and your managers is that you all need to inspire a lot of people to carefully orchestrate these projects in a coordinated way. Everyone needs to understand both the big picture and their individual roles and tasks to be successful as a team; thus, the why, what, and how.

7—Spirit of Growth

This is a value that I personally adopted early in life. I often refer to myself as a lifelong learner, and I wanted to bring this into the culture of our organization. My personal belief was that some of the "why" behind what we were doing was for the growth and the experience alone. Yes, our spin-off occurred as a result of the US stock market crash in 2008 and 2009, and we were trying to save our company; however, I wanted the team to be as excited as I was about all the personal growth the spin-off effort would allow us.

Not everyone on your team will catch "growth fever." Not everyone who starts the project with you will be able to adapt and adjust to the new culture. Even still I encourage you to embrace this value.

There will be a day when one of the leaders or a rock-star independent contributor is not able to succeed in the new company. You will need to make a tough decision and have a difficult discussion with them about their performance. If you've adopted this value, you have done everything you can to support and help the person grow and be successful in their role. You can still feel good about yourself and your role in their growth even if you need to let them go.

This belief almost became a mantra for me throughout my career. I couldn't guarantee that someone would always have employment at the firm where I was a manager or leader. However, I could guarantee, to the best of my capability, that they would have a better skillset from having worked with me.

Strive to be a giving and coaching leader. This helps with empowerment but also builds the loyalty of your team.

8—"We Are They!"

This concept also isn't from a book. This is something that I created because I had an ah-ha moment early on in the first spin-off.

From my experience, both in life and at work, there is always the elusive "they" who make decisions, set strategy, determine budgets, approve purchasing requests, and determine corporate standards and policies. In life, "they" create the rules, set laws, and enforce them.

To create a culture of empowerment, you'll need to try and break through the limiting belief that someone else is in charge. I needed to overcome this belief myself, and it was the ah-ha of realizing that I personally needed to set the tone and the culture of my organization that resulted in this "We are they!" concept.

The general idea is that when you spin off and become your own firm, there is no longer a group of decision-makers somewhere off at "corporate" setting strategy, making decisions, and creating rules. Now you and your leaders are "the ones."

Independence is exciting, but it can also be a scary endeavor. There is no more "they." You and your direct reports are the highest technology managers of the firm. You will make decisions, set strategy, approve purchases, and determine standards and policies. I've purposely left budgets out of this second list because there is likely a board who has final approval authority on large financial decisions, but for the rest, the entire executive team and the board are looking at you as the technology leader to drive all things tech-related.

It should start to sink in. To help your team reach the level of empowerment to be successful and to get everyone to operate with the level of autonomy and ownership you are striving for, help them embrace the "We are they!" concept. Let them know this is a driver for the culture you are trying to create, and be sure to reinforce the need to ask empowering questions.

Your leadership team must embrace this concept to carry the culture changes throughout the organization. They need to embody the values, behaviors, and beliefs that you are trying to instill. This culture will eventually resonate with your leaders and should result in everyone understanding that everyone together is in charge of your organization's destiny.

Train Your Leaders

Once you have defined the culture you'd like to build, you have to educate your organization and start the process of rolling it out, so you can see the team and leaders embody the essence of what you want.

This is not the easy task. Defining the culture is easy, while the roll-out takes purpose and time.

In addition to the mandatory weekly meetings mentioned earlier in the book, here are three things I've done to build the new culture. I highly recommend that you use all of them. Adopting them may push you out of your comfort zone, as it did for me, so seize any discomfort here as an opportunity for more growth. There are experts at leading organizational change that you can hire, but this is possible to do yourself.

1—Weekly Leaders Meetings

There is not going to be a lot of time to send your leaders to formal training, but they still need to be trained. I have to admit, this was one of my favorite parts! Now that I have gotten a formal certification as a coach and see that I have a passion for helping and growing others, it makes sense. At the time, I just thought maybe I was a little zealous.

I had a weekly mandatory leaders meeting in addition to the all-hands meeting. This meeting included all extended leaders in the organization, anyone who had supervisor-level responsibility. Some of the managers hated this. Most of the feedback I received was very positive.

This weekly leaders meeting was to set the tone, culture, and roll-out of my shared vision and to educate the supervisors in the organization on what I expected from them and how I expected them to behave.

I created presentations and trained them on most of the eight secret weapons, given in this chapter, I use to establish a culture of empowerment.

In the bonus website for this book, I'm offering videos in which I'm delivering some of this training. You can download the presentations and deliver them yourself, or have your managers watch my delivery. I don't expect to have these videos completed by the initial publication of the book, but keep looking and they will appear as I develop them.

Here's the site: **www.howtoleadacorporatespinoff.com/bonuses**

2—Reading Club

Another trick to help reinforce the culture you want to build is to buy all the leaders on your team one or more of the above books and then give them a month to read the book. Set a discussion date in one of the weekly leaders meetings and have a management book club. To run the reading club, you can get a list of questions from the internet for each one of the books you choose. I found just a few questions was all that was needed to spark a dialogue and conversation.

Again, this was received well by most of the leaders when I implemented it, but there were a couple of complainers. Not so ironically, the group of complainers were also nay-sayers. There are likely to be some people on your team who think all this "soft stuff" is a waste of time and that everyone is a professional, so everyone should just do their jobs. The way to motivate people is to make them feel they are valued and part of the team. It requires making them do things that are good for them, not necessarily what they like to do.

3—Culture Changes in Performance Objectives

I am assuming that you have a formal process for setting goals and objectives for the annual performance review. The best way to get the managers to execute and roll out the values and behaviors that you want is to add this to those objectives. Creating an objective that is ten to twenty-five percent of their performance rating for the year and attaching their bonus to their ability to be successful in the new culture is a very effective way to see the changes you want.

Watch-Outs

I mentioned before that not everyone who was with you at the legacy firm will be comfortable with the new culture you are trying to create. Some of them won't be successful or transition well into this new environment. Pay attention to who is struggling. If they cannot be the leader you need them to be, you're best to make the necessary changes quickly and bring in a different leader who is a better long-term fit.

Changing the culture of a firm is difficult. It requires re-invention; not only of the firm and the leaders, but of yourself. The focus needed to be an example and embody empowerment can be supported by hiring an executive coach or mentor to give you feedback, encouragement and moral support.

This is also an area that I can and am willing to help you with. This chapter has a lot of information in it. I am providing videos in the bonus materials that come with the book to help explain some of the topics, but I am also available for consulting and coaching on organizational change, not just strategy review and planning. As mentioned before, you will find my contact information on the copyright page.

To repeat, my intention is to develop the bonus content for this book over time, so check the site regularly for the most recent additions: **www.howtoleadacorporatespinoff.com/bonuses.**

Up Next

Just as the right culture permeates the whole organization to create a positive and highly functional environment, so does well-considered communication. The next chapter addresses seven (well, really eight) communication characteristics that when in place, sow the seeds for an approachable, inclusive, and high-functioning workplace.

12.

Foster Excellent Communication

In the real estate world, they say it's all about "location, location, location." I say for a successful spin-off you need "communication, communication, communication." Over time, I created what we called the "Seven Cs." This was an easy tagline that I came up with to create a culture of communication. The idea is to share it with the entire organization and try to foster a culture of excellent communicators. My Seven Cs do work! I still get calls and texts from managers in my old organizations when they decide it's time to share the Seven Cs with their group.

There are a lot of excellent books on communication. The Seven Cs is how I summarized it for my team. It's short, simple, and sweet. And it works! After brainstorming with the leaders of the organization on this a few times, every other month or so, I had a leader in the organization get in front of the department in one of our mandatory meetings and re-train on this list of Seven Cs. The goal was to have all the leaders own it. Over time it was fun to see people print out this list and hang it up in their cubicles. Eventually, IT managers were sharing it with their business partners, and it spread further into the organization organically.

Repetition is the mother of all skill.

—TONY ROBBINS

1—Clear

If you want to have clear and strong communication skills, you need to understand upfront what it is you are trying to communicate. You have to match your style to your message. For instance, before engaging with someone, to make sure you are clear on what you want to say, you can ask yourself the following: "What is the reason for the communication? Is it about giving someone information, an 'FYI,' or am I trying to get their buy-in? Another option: am I setting the stage for decision-making? Or am I just aiming to brainstorm with them?" Other than actually socializing, these are the primary reasons for communication at work.

To be a great communicator, the best thing to do is to tell your audience, upfront, what kind of message you're trying to impart. For example, you could walk into the boss's office and begin by saying, "Hey, I need to brainstorm with you for a minute. I'm not looking for a decision or raising an issue. I just need your expertise and want to brainstorm with you." Or you might say, "Something's come up. There's an issue. Here is some information around the facts that you should know about." By identifying the reason you are communicating, the resulting exchange is more focused and clear for both you and the receiver.

You might need to win somebody over to your side of a debate. In that case, you will need negotiation and persuasion skills. You will need to describe the facts and all the reasons, the pros and cons, of the position that you have. If you are setting the stage for decision-making, you will need an executive summary of the issue or the decision that is needed. You'll need to highlight all of the critical analysis points needed for decision-making. You should bullet out the pros, cons, and costs associated with the decision, and you'll need to time-box the discussion.

If you can be very clear upfront on the purpose of the dialogue, you're not only setting the stage for your communication style, but you will also be putting the receiver in the right state of mind.

2—Concise

One of the things I've observed is that team members can be uncomfortable communicating with more senior-level people. Just being around senior-level people can make them nervous. This manifests itself in rambling and going on and on in their communication style, often taking a long time to get to their point.

I teach people to be not only clear but also concise, avoiding over-communicating by delivering just the right amount of information needed for the dialogue. Try to eliminate all the "extra" stuff and the story that seeps into the dialogue. Don't, for example, walk someone through all twenty hours of analysis that has been done, but rather present the conclusions. Yes, be clear on why you arrived there and what you'll be saying, but only give context to the overall situation and be as succinct as possible.

3—Confident

Thinking about the fear some people have in communicating within an organization, it's important to help them come across as confident. It's easier to appear confident when you are prepared and have done your homework. This means doing a thorough analysis and an evaluation of the pros and cons of a recommendation if required, and/or preparing a set of key points that you want to communicate. Once the prep work is complete, the speaker can focus on the key messages that they aim to communicate, rather than who the message is being presented to. If the focus is on the message and the analysis work is thorough, then you will come to the table prepared, confident, and able to express yourself better.

4—Control

"Control" is more about a communication style. It is often thought of as being close to coming across as confident. However, showing "control" is really about being calm, slow, and deliberate in your delivery. Not coming across as if you are rushed. You need to avoid the mistake of acting like everything is an emergency. Instead, you and your team should focus on delivering facts and information, not feelings or gut reactions without any analysis.

There will be times when your team members are overwhelmed and flat-out afraid because of the pace at which they will need to work. You may hear them say, "That's impossible. We can't do it." I recommend that you respond to them, saying something such as, "Take a breath and relax for a minute. Gather some more facts and information. Then let's analyze what's true and what's not true. Let's put some control around this."

5—In Charge

This is aligned with creating a leadership culture. I tried to teach everyone regardless of their role, that to appear as leaders, we needed to understand that a large part of that centers on others' perceptions around how we communicate. If you are practicing these communication tools, you will come across as in charge. It doesn't mean bossy, it doesn't mean you're running around telling everybody what to do, but rather you are in control of your delivery. When you are in control of your delivery, you are perceived to be a leader. You are a leader.

6—InClusive

This is one of the most important skills: being inclusive. You want to teach everyone in your organization to constantly ask themselves, and each other, "Who else needs to know this? Who can benefit from this information? Is this urgent and should we send out an FYI communication, so people feel like they know what's going on and to bring others up to speed?"

Getting the team to own and understand they have a responsibility in communicating with others and in helping everyone understand the status of things is critical to the overall success of the spin-off. It is critical to remember to include not only other employees in the organization, but also any temporary resources brought on the team to help with the project and any external partners that you have hired. Communication is often overlooked, so be good at it and you will be seen as a natural leader.

7—Close the Loop

This is the last of the original Seven Cs, and it surfaced because of a pet peeve of mine. In my organization, I needed to enforce this message that just because you send an email to somebody, it does not mean that your role and responsibility is complete. To be an outstanding communicator, there needs to be a lot of follow-ups. If someone has not confirmed or responded, you cannot assume that the message was received. You are responsible for closing the loop and making sure that your message was actually delivered. If you have not received a response, it could have gone to junk mail, or it could have reached them while they were out of the office and ended up overlooked. You must close the loop with somebody if they haven't responded. There are many ways people can close the loop: a phone call, a text, a follow-up email, or a face-to-face discussion in the hallway or in a meeting.

The 8th C—Collaboration

We didn't start off with this one, but over time I realized it belongs on the list. Being willing to work with others and not be an independent island is one of the most important habits. Getting people to move out from behind their email and screens to start collaborating with each other face-to-face can be very difficult in an IT organization.

I know a lot of people on your team will think that everyone can get things done more efficiently with email, but nothing solves issues like brainstorming and collaborating face-to-face with other people in the department. So, although this isn't necessarily a communication style, it's a cultural trait that I added on in terms of fostering a culture that supports good communication.

SECTION BRIEF

In section 2 "People," we've looked at how you can see, support, and lead your people through the separation and spin-off. Remember, this includes both your longtime colleagues as well as your new hires, temporary and long-term. The culture you grow, both amongst the leadership team and amongst all employees, plays a huge role in the level of success the spin-off effort and new organization will experience. Be thoughtful and communicative, and teach everyone else to be so too. It goes a long way.

As a reminder, I am including a set of bonus materials with this book at **www.howtoleadacorporatespinnoff.com/bonuses** where I have provided both videos of myself delivering these points and where I share presentation materials.

I am available to come on location at your organization and help train your leadership team by working with you to create a custom curriculum of any of this information if you think it will be of help. We can work together to define the culture you'd like to build, and we can create a one- or two-day leadership meeting to get your leadership team on board and trained. As mentioned in several other chapters of this book, you will find my contact information on the copyright page.

Up Next

Section 3 "Program Management" should help you consider important aspects of the new project that you'll be running. Risk reduction, response to unanticipated problems, and levels of support you can expect from your parent company are on our agenda for discussion. We will begin the new section by addressing how you can divide the whole mammoth effort into separate, manageable workstreams.

PROGRAM MANAGEMENT

13.

Divide the Program into Multiple Workstreams

After reading the first two sections, you created a list of services and assessed the skills you have on your team. You brought more of your team into the loop and shared with them some of the information about what is ahead for all of you.

If you feel a little overwhelmed, it's natural. In this section, we are going to break down all the work into a set of projects and then deconstruct it even further into a series of efforts that can be run somewhat independently. Your project will be different and not the same set of services that I describe below. However, all IT departments consist of similar components, so you will find a lot to leverage in this section.

First, I recommend thinking of the separation project as a large program or set of projects. Once you make the program into this defined set of initiatives or workstreams, as I call them, suddenly the effort will seem more manageable for everyone! You have the list of projects and can determine if any of the efforts seem more difficult than others and then prioritize the order by which you will start the vendor selection efforts.

As soon as you settle on the set of workstreams and structure for your program, it's time to start communicating to the organization how the separation effort is to be driven. The more communication, the better. All employees will be impacted, so calming them down early, answering questions, and communicating timeframes along the way are important.

As you read my thoughts on the structure below, remember that you can hire project and program management skills for all of these workstreams. The infrastructure leader, the security officer, and the service desk manager who will be able to operate these business functions after separation is not the same person who will be good at driving the projects.

I suggest the following workstreams are required to transition IT to a standalone company:

- Data center conversion, modernization, and management
- Network and telephony
- Employee productivity—hardware and software
- Corporate applications
- Marketing and digital services
- Compliance and regulatory applications
- Vendor contract management
- Operational readiness

For the rest of the chapter, I'll go into each of these in more detail.

Data Center Conversion, Modernization, and Management

The only way you might not have this workstream in your program is if you've already been running as an independent, standalone entity. You may be running in your own data center and on all your own hardware. If this is the case, this workstream may only involve reviewing your service and any contracts you have in place to deliver this to your organization. If the contracts are under the parent company's legal entity, it's time to repaper and renegotiate the terms and SLAs.

On both of the spin-offs I was involved with, this was the largest workstream and had the longest implementation time. I am assuming that your division runs in a corporate data center or a corporate-provided managed data center. You and your team are charged with finding a new data center, building out all the hardware, migrating all your applications and data to that new facility, and standing up all operations, service, support, and maintenance for the application portfolio in that new data center.

You will want to use this opportunity to modernize the architecture and address any availability issues, disaster recovery, and business continuity gaps. You'll want to formalize service restoration processes and identify the maintenance and server patching schedules that will best meet your business objectives. There are many firms out there to help your data center modernization efforts. This is a place to apply the example of hiring strategy consultants to help you select a new data center facility or managed service provider. There are consultants and consulting firms that are available to help you do the selection process and negotiate the overall service contract. If you go the managed service provider route, these contracts can be long and complex, so having an expert on hand to help you navigate it can save you from some costly mistakes.

Remember to add penalties or bonuses to the contract to incentivize the vendor to meet the implementation dates and to keep the project implementation team on hand for at least thirty days after going live.

A critical tip for a smoother execution of this workstream is to include your application support team throughout the entire process. Although your team of application managers likely doesn't have much experience in selecting and picking a data center, they will be one hundred percent involved with this workstream, and they will be migrating all their applications to the new environment. You can't do this project without the managers. I highly recommend that you try as much as possible to eliminate the number of existing projects that are on their plates so that they can focus just on this effort. Involving them in the vendor selection process and having them work side-by-side with the consulting firm is critical to identifying all the technical requirements.

There are many "warts" to uncover in your portfolio as part of this project. I am confident that once you get under the covers on the application portfolio, there will be several instances of applications that were running both on unsupported software and unsupported operating systems. Having your team of managers actively engaged will help identify these types of issues early in the project. If you are running on unsupported operating systems, you should have the teams upgrade in place and test the stability of the applications before you move them to a new data center.

Network and Telephony

This workstream starts off sounding easy and straightforward, but there are many complexities. You should think about them early as you assign project team members to this effort. First, there is the network and the MPLS. I am assuming that you have multiple locations and are not collocated with your data center. There are a

LOT of providers in this space. For every connection, you need a backup. You will be working with Verizon, CenturyLink, Quest, and other last-mile providers that are local to you.

There are many consultants and strategists in this space, thankfully. They will tell you that this work only takes ninety days. I have not seen a project that proves this yet. Scheduling with the providers and coordinating dates and times for the work to be done in parallel is always a challenge. You'll need to design and architect how your locations will connect to each other and to the data center and how the telephony system will work on top of that network as well. I've seen both models where all internal phone traffic goes into the data center first and then back out to a different location and locations having their own equipment, making point-to-point location calls possible.

Not only is coordination with the providers complex, but cutover activities from the old systems to the new one requires laying your new network down in parallel to the one that is already in place. This involves a lot of physical work in the locations and hands-on support to run the network out to the desks. Phone drops are easier, but you will need to determine if you must purchase all new equipment or if you are able to assume ownership of the equipment already in place. These details will change the strategy of the cutover.

The biggest complexity with the phone system conversion is usually when you are using call centers and hunt groups. Every 800 number in the firm needs to be identified, as well as the call queues associated with the number and the list of agents that are assigned to each queue. If there are rules about which phones should ring if someone doesn't answer a call, your team will need to document these rules, and then they will be programmed into the new system. A dry run and testing of all the phones, the caller id from each line, the call groups, the 800 number, and the call recording equipment is required. The go-live for this project can take an army of people over a weekend. There is a lot of organizational communication needed in this workstream, so planning early is important.

Employee Productivity—Hardware and Software

The employees of the organization may think that the spin-off doesn't impact them or their jobs, at first, but when you start to explain to them all the changes ahead, you will start to get many questions. This workstream is a broad category that encompasses all the hardware and software that employees use at their desktops in their day-to-day job functions. I've included a bullet list of the areas of change that were involved in my two projects. The extent of this list and the number of changes will be unique to your situation.

- IT service desk and desktop support
- Hardware refresh/replacement—printers, faxes, laptops, desktops, and mobile device management
- Software and license purchasing and management
- File share services—file shares, SharePoint, local storage, and backup
- Corporate collaboration tools—chat, email
- Security fulfillment and access management

These are the projects that impact everyone. You may or may not need to replace all the hardware, but if you are using very dated equipment, a refresh of the computers might be required. Don't underestimate the amount of time and testing it takes to create a new standard desktop build that you will use to roll out to the organization. All applications will need to be retested on the new build before you can begin, and the process that you will use to transfer all the employee data from each person's old machine to the new one is cumbersome and time-consuming.

Policies related to the service desk and all the workflow associated with handling the issues and tickets created as the employees report problems with their new equipment need to be defined upfront and communicated to the organization ahead of time to have a smooth transition. In the section on operational readiness, you will find a list of the processes that you should expect to create.

Corporate Applications—Payroll, Human Resources Tools, General Ledger, and Procurement

Although the data center modernization and migration project will be the most complicated and the longest effort for your organization, there can be an equal amount of urgency to start the separation and the implementation of your own set of corporate applications. The overall tone for this set of applications is that it is typically needed ASAP, so your firm can have independence in this area as quickly as possible.

I've found that HR is usually driving the pace of this initiative more than finance because, as you've seen, the path to independence involves hiring a lot of talent. That won't only be in the technology department. HR is trying to support all departments in this effort, so getting production on their own payroll system, standing up benefits, and formalizing hiring and onboarding practices are their focus. There are a lot of consultants in this space, both individuals and companies, to help you select either a bundled solution for the enterprise or independent solutions that you integrate.

I recommend that you look at the bundled packages and that you find a cloud solution. ADP, Oracle, Workday, and others in this space have all improved dramatically in the last few years. Each of them started with a niche area and then bolted on other capabilities through either development or acquiring other firms to create bundled solutions. As you build your list of requirements from HR and finance, you will find that some of the products are more favored by HR and others more favored by finance. I'd try to meet the senior leaders of each group and get their buy-in to a bundled package if possible.

That said, I have implemented systems in this space several times in my career, and only the largest companies that can afford the top-of-the-line solutions have ever implemented a full-service provider. Most of the mid-size companies need to implement less costly solutions and are left integrating more "right-size" products. Still, you will find many consultants and strategists to help find and define your project and vendors. You will find many niche consultants who are finance or HR implementation specialists. Expect to pay top dollar on consultants in this space. They are in high demand and charge a lot. Just check their references. You will find differently sized partners are targeting different sized firms. Try to find one experienced with working at implementations that are the same ballpark size as yours.

I have worked on several projects to implement HR and payroll, twice in the last few years. The first time we used the implementation team of the product vendor we selected, and the second time we used an implementation partner of the product vendor. My overall recommendation on this workstream is to use as few partners as possible. Working with two different firms had a series of challenges that could be the topic of an entire book. I can give you consulting advice and coaching on this decision privately if you'd like to learn more. Remember you can find my contact information on the copyright page.

Marketing and Digital Services

There are many technology platforms in the marketing group. Most of them are in the cloud at this point. I listed some of the tools and services here to help you initiate a dialogue with the CMO. The marketing department will likely have their own project manager running their pieces of the spin-off, but sometimes these are the tech leader's responsibility. It's best to understand the plan for the social media management tools, content management and marketing systems, advertising tools and software, customer relationship management, website management, and domain management. Most of these tools will be cloud-based and require price negotiation, transfer or purchase of licenses, data conversions, and new contracts. I would recommend that you don't use this project as the time to "convert" from one provider to another if it can be avoided.

Compliance and Regulatory Applications

Because every industry is different, your compliance and regulatory application portfolio will depend on that industry. Common needs include email surveillance, email archive, and discovery tools. A conversation with your chief compliance officer or corporate information security officer, if you have people in these roles, will help define the scope of the work.

Vendor Contract Management

You will be able to operate with most vendors and software providers for a period of time under the transition services agreement. However, the legal team needs to be prepared. Every contract, vendor, software license provider, and agreement will need to be reviewed and likely rewritten on the letterhead of the new legal entity. Naming someone in the technology department to begin drafting the list of contracts and providers is important.

Operational Readiness

This is the most overlooked set of activities and will be the downfall of your project if you don't hire or assign someone to drive this effort. Thinking about what the operational processes will be for the organization after you are spun off and independent is the last item on everyone's mind. It takes focused energy and attention to ensure this is prepared for. This workstream is mandatory. You already operate with processes at the parent firm, but simplifying these is likely needed. When you add all new partners and vendors, these processes naturally need to be revisited. Some of the vendors you hire will have their own tools and methods for executing. Try to learn about these capabilities upfront in the RFP process.

The critical processes the organization needs to define as part of the service desk include all of the following:

- desktop support and maintenance
- ordering, replacing, and approving the purchase of hardware and software licenses
- requesting and approving application access
- onboarding of new employees, transfers, and termination of employees
- incident and change management
- server patching, OS upgrading/maintenance
- security patching
- security incidents
- business continuity and disaster recovery
- data center failover and failback activities
- network and telephone failover and failback activities

I must repeat: it will be the downfall of your project if you don't hire or assign someone to drive this effort of preparing for your operational readiness.

Up Next

Now that you've divided the separation effort into distinct workstreams, you are in a great position to determine cost estimates, both for the separation execution and the annual budget for running the new organization. That's the focus of the next chapter.

14.

Estimate the Effort

You may find that the company purchasing your firm will ask you, the CIO, to estimate the cost of (1) the separation project and (2) the annual budget to run the new organization on an ongoing basis. These numbers are used to run their models and determine a purchase price. Typically, the request will occur before you have selected any vendors. This can be your earliest challenge, but with the list of projects created from the previous section, you are halfway there.

The Spreadsheet Approach

When I was asked to make this cost estimate, I used a spreadsheet approach. While it created a false sense of precision, it also gave me confidence in the numbers I was proposing. For every project identified, we listed all the possible roles and determined how many months each role would be engaged in the effort. We then calculated an expected rate for an incremental resource in this role to work full-time for a month. We ran the calculation, summed up the total, and applied a confidence factor of multiplying the final cost by 1.25 to 1.5 to create a cost range. Just remember to round the numbers at the end of the process, so it is clear these are estimates. I recommend rounding to the nearest $25,000.

The T-Shirt Size Approach

An alternative approach that we matured to after a couple of years was to just "t-shirt size" each project with a standard set of assumptions. For example, a "small" would have half of a project manager, a full-time technical lead, a full-time business analyst, and a tester. This "small" effort would run for three months. Then we applied the monthly incremental rates for the roles and came up with a standard cost range for each size: x-small, small, medium, large, and jumbo. Again, even in this approach, multiply your final numbers by 1.25 and 1.5 to create a range and then round to the nearest $25,000.

The Annual Budget

Calculating the annual operating budget is more difficult. It requires some broad assumptions and a detailed analysis of the current state financials. It's a similar exercise as estimating the separation cost, but here you'll be listing out all the departments in the organization and getting swags for your end state:

- Labor (the number of employees on your team)
- Hardware (based on the number of employees in the organization and also the annual expense based on the size of the application portfolio and the number of servers you are projecting in your footprint)
- Estimated service provider expenses
- Annual software licensing and maintenance fees

These are broad categories, but it will get you started.

One hidden component of the operational budget that you should be aware of is that there will be a period when you are beginning to have new expenses, but you're not ready to give notice to the legacy parent company that you are ready to terminate services. This is what we referred to as the "bubble cost." Year one operational expenses are higher because you will be operating and paying for two organizational platforms until you are ready to sever service. The bubble cost can be a driving factor in your staggered implementation strategy and rollout plan. As services go live, you can terminate them from the parent and, therefore, reduce the overall expense.

The Hundred-Plus Questions

Once you submit your estimates, it is very likely that the company that is purchasing you will hire independent contractors and consulting companies to analyze your assumptions. This process is difficult, and they ask hundreds of questions over and over. Expect to be asked to walk through every aspect of each workstream on your strategy approach, estimates, and assumptions. They will challenge you on everything. Their role is to give the firm that hired them an accurate estimate.

I didn't know until several years later, after the fact, that our purchaser assumed that our estimates were optimistic, and they added six months to the forecast and used the monthly run rate to calculate a different number for use in their modeling.

I do think that you can spin off your organization within a one-year timeframe from the date of close. Your belief that it can be done and confidence in your strategy make for a huge influencer for the effort. Whatever timeframe it is that you think the project is going to take, add at least three or four months to your estimate. Again, if this sounds complicated, it's not meant to be.

Contact me through my email on the copyright page and we can talk about how I might be able to provide support.

Up Next

In the next chapter, I present you eleven areas to consider, so you can minimize the overall risk in this huge and exciting spin-off effort.

15.

Reduce Risks

This spin-off effort entails a lot of risks. However, with careful planning, good communication, the right partners, and the right people on your team—what we've talked about in sections 1 and 2—you've set the stage for a lot of things to go right. Let's talk about how to minimize the overall risk.

1. Risk reduction—Freeze out other IT projects.

Try to freeze other IT projects if possible. It won't be possible to stop all efforts, but the fewer initiatives that are on your plate, the better. It allows everyone to focus. Production support is always required, so you should consider dedicating resources to that task and diverting all others to the separation effort.

2. Risk reduction—Hire experts.

Hire experts rather than trying to learn as you go. We've already examined the importance of having the right people and having the right partners. In the spirit of repetition, you may have very high-talent employees on your team, but you all just don't have the luxury of time to learn on the job. There are too many moving components and too many new skills to ramp up fast. It's better to have experts, either on hand for the project duration, or have a couple of experts on retainer that you can call on when you get yourself into some trouble.

3. Risk reduction—Establish the right governance.

A lot of people think that governance means administration overhead. There are a lot of issues that surface during this project and a lot of decisions that must be made every day, hour by hour. These decisions can have a ripple effect across multiple workstreams. There can be unintended consequences, and if there are some teams that are operating with a decision that is just a few hours behind the new latest direction, they could be wasting time on something that they shouldn't be doing. When governance is set up correctly, it's about giving the team access to the decision-makers quickly and as soon as possible.

Each of the workstreams should have a separate steering committee, and there should be a separate program-level steering committee as well. Steering committee meetings should be scheduled once a week, but in crunch time as you get close to implementation, you will likely need daily huddles with steering committee leaders and the project leaders within the whole program.

4. Risk reduction—Aim for a speedy separation.

Separate as quickly as possible. The longer the transition services agreement (TSA), the more difficult and contentious the relationship with the legacy firm can be.

5. Risk reduction—Do a careful TSA negotiation.

Negotiate the TSA carefully and insist on an extension clause. Everyone has the same goal—to have this project run smoothly, without issue, and as quickly as possible—but issues can occur and force you to extend the TSA for one or more services. That's why you must negotiate the TSA carefully and insist on an extension clause.

6. Risk reduction—Divide the costs in the TSA for each IT service area.

Divide the TSA into a cost for each of the IT service areas. An example is to get the cost for the network and telephones, data center management, desktop services, and email, each as individual items. The reason for doing this is to enable a staged implementation plan and shut these services down one at a time.

7. Risk reduction—Right-size the application portfolio.

The IT tools, products, and software that were used at the parent company may be too large and expensive for your new organization. You are a smaller firm and won't have the same pricing leverage as before. You'll have to ensure that you aren't over-engineered with products you cannot operationally afford over the long term. This may require replacing databases, such as Oracle or DB2 with SQLServer, or the use of open-source solutions instead of market leaders with high expense in each category. The point is to minimize your expense risk by choosing right-size applications and software.

8. Risk reduction—Go for a stage-approached implementation of new services.

Implement your new services in a staged approach rather than a "big-bang" switch to the new capabilities. I sometimes refer to this approach as the "ratchet-down strategy" as well because you are slowly staging and implementing things for your new organization and spinning off from the parent while you are ratcheting down the services purchased in the TSA agreement.

You should approach every project by asking if its particular services could go first. Can you do an email conversion early? Can you get the phone system delivered first? Can you build out your network before you do your data center migration? Can you bundle or unbundle your application portfolio into groups or waves? This strategy is all about removing false dependencies across projects.

9. Risk reduction—Select an implementation date and time that will have the least business disruption.

In many industries, business hours are twenty-four hours a day and seven days a week. This makes implementation of new technology and service provider cut-over activities high risk. In the financial services industry where I've had all of my experience implementing change, we always selected weekends as the best time to reduce the disruption to the business. The stock market is closed, and we usually had a low number of employees working on the weekends. Weekends give you at least forty-eight hours to work through all your implementation tasks. I've found that you need all those hours even on very practiced implementations. If your implementation can fall on a three-day holiday weekend, that will further reduce risk by giving your team even more time to address issues if any occur during the implementation.

10. Risk reduction—Practice, practice, practice to get it right.

Execute dry runs. This approach is about practicing until it's perfect. You should have your teams practice all the data and application migration activities exactly as you would execute the day-by-day, hour-by-hour, step-by-step implementation plans and give the entire plan a dry run. The dry run should include both the rollout and the back-out plans. A critical task during the dry runs is to identify what I call the "point of no return."

There is a point in the timeline during the implementation plan that if you haven't gotten to all of the tasks that you're supposed to at that certain point in the plan, you need to stop moving forward, declare the project a no-go, and start executing the rollback. To define this critical milestone, the team will need to know exactly how long the rollback will take. With this number, you subtract from the go-live launch timeline so that you know what time "the point of no return" occurs. Then you have to test in the dry run that you can execute all of your implementation tasks within the time from when the plan starts until the time of the point of no return. This process not only helps you identify critical timelines within the implementation plan, it also identifies any missing tasks in your planning itself. I recommend that you test not only the implementation plan, but also the step-by-step back-out plan and practice the communication needed for the actual implementation as well in the dry run.

11. Risk reduction—Have several extensive reviews with your teams.

Have regular project plan deep dives with the teams to keep them on track. In Section 2 on People, I mentioned that some leadership books advise you to pick the right people and get out of their way. However, this project is not the right time for that. The risks are too high, and you are responsible and accountable for everything that goes wrong. I highly recommend intense line-by-line reviews of the project plan. Understand what the teams are doing, what their assumptions are, and determine if there are any missing steps and components. I recommend that you do this with somebody who has run one of these programs before. If you can hire outside help or an independent review, that is best. Outside help can identify potential risks and interdependencies that the team may not have seen.

A deep dive is required at several points throughout the project life cycle. You will want the initial deep dive meeting as the teams put together their strategy and game plan. Have a second deep dive aligned at the same time as you kick off testing. This second extensive review with your team will identify all the outstanding development tasks.

I recommend doing a third deep dive review just before the teams put together their hour-by-hour implementation plans and before you start executing the dry run. This starts the process for preparing and identifying the implementation dates.

Up Next

Even with all the forethought and planning to minimize risks, the reality is that issues will arise. In the next chapter, I give advice on how to proceed when you find an issue.

16.

Resolve Issues

Regardless of how great your planning processes are, how experienced the consultants are that you brought in to help you, and the amount of risk you considered and worked to minimize, things will go wrong. For example, the amount of time you need to complete all the tasks just won't fit in the needed window of time available; a critical resource on the project suddenly gets sick and is hospitalized without a backup; or it's possible that you decided to send the data physically on an airplane with an employee and their luggage containing the hard drives goes missing . . .

I'm not trying to scare you or be a defeatist. I simply want you to be prepared because it's the reality of what happens. Each of these above examples actually occurred in one of my spin-off projects. You can't predict everything, and you can't plan around every scenario. So what should you do when an issue arises?

Step 1—Stay calm and assess.

The first step to solving any issue is not to immediately panic. It may be hard to do. After a few issues arise, you might start doubting that the spin-off is ever going to finish. Just stay calm and start working to assess the impact. Ask yourself, "What is the resulting effect regarding the timeline, budget, critical functionality, and capability?"

Step 2—Invite others to assess with you.

If you have senior-level resources on the team, I recommend bringing them in for a brainstorming session. Look at the issue together, even if it occurs on a part of the project they are not involved in. The more thought power, the better. Consider if you should bring in the employees working on that particular part of the effort as well because there are probably people on that team who know the right response and action, but they are, for whatever reason, not bringing it up.

Be honest with yourself based on the assessment. So often, we are invested in getting the spin-off done on time and on budget that we have a blind spot related to how an issue could impact us. You might even have a manager on your team who refuses to believe there's an issue, so you need to deliver an honest, detached assessment of the situation.

Step 3—Make some lists and do some rankings.

Create a list of scenarios, plans, alternative options, and choices for resolving the issue. Remind yourself of all the strategists available on retainer for an outsider perspective. As the team documents the issue and their ideas to address it, you capture the pros and cons, the cost, and the time each of the scenarios would take. Rank the options in priority order from best to least best-case scenario.

Step 4—Share the issue with your boss and executive leaders.

Now take this list to your boss, and tell them there is an issue. As the new CIO, you may be reluctant to communicate the problem as you will feel like every step and move you make is being evaluated. Any mistake will feel more significant than it is.

You must remember: every project will have issues; it's how you handle a problem when it occurs that is the indication of who you are as a leader. Open, transparent, and early communication about the issue and the different scenarios available are important.

After talking with your boss, I recommend bringing the scenarios to the executive team for transparency and discussion. It is possible that these leaders will have viable workarounds that are acceptable to the business and that will allow you to fix the issue after you go live.

My Story of an Issue

I had one issue at our separation from ING that felt horrible and devastating. Here's that story.

When we replaced all of the laptops and desktops for the employees and contractors, we installed a new version of Windows onto the machines that none of the employees had experience using. On top of that, we added security and encryption software that added complexity to the login and start-up process. These brand-new machines would spontaneously reboot themselves or get hit with the blue screen of death multiple times a day.

The stability issues were very frustrating to the employees, especially those in the call center answering phones for clients. A short period after the rollout, our customers started to let on that this instability was impacting them because they were beginning to hear complaints from our employees. After a conversation with the rest of the executive team, we delivered some key communication to the employees.

We communicated that while we in IT were working as fast as we could to resolve the issues, we asked the employees not to express to our customers the trouble they were having. This wasn't the best scenario, but overall it created an environment that at least internalized some of the early issues. It gave the IT department a little bit of space to tell everybody we knew that there were systemic issues with the laptops and were working to resolve them.

The takeaway: when issues surface, get back in front of your team. The people on the team probably already know about it. They have been informally talking about it in the hallway (or, in my case, with customers . . .). I would be willing to wager that the employees have known there has been an issue for a couple weeks.

As soon as you are aware of the issue and you've put together scenarios and communicated with the senior executives of the firm, get in front of your team to describe the different resolution strategies and how you're going to handle it. The important thing is to have everyone understand that everything is under control and you're working to resolve things. These types of problems can create a little bit of a frenzy in the organization, and you are trying to avoid that.

Up Next

Speaking of issues, something that will certainly come up is how much support, if any, you can expect from your parent legacy company. That's the subject of the next chapter.

17.

Consider the Helpfulness of the Legacy Firm

What support can you depend on from your legacy parent company? This is a totally fair question to ask, and the answer will depend on them as well as some other factors that we'll cover in this chapter.

As I mentioned in chapter one, the level of support I had early on to assist in setting a strategic partner strategy was non-existent. I was on my own. However, I did have a manager who suggested I put together a funding plan to hire the consulting firm to help with the vendor selection processes. This small amount of support and advice was what I needed to get moving.

Throughout both of the spinoffs projects I was involved with, there were varying levels of support throughout the efforts. A team of people at the legacy firm will be assigned to work with you to make the project a success. However, know that the cooperation and assistance does vary.

The People Factor

If your legacy parent company has experience running divestitures, then they will come to the table with ideas and strategies on how to execute this kind of project. If the divestiture is new, then everyone will be learning together with you. Either way, the level of cooperation will largely depend on the people at the parent company that you are assigned to work with.

The politics involved with trying to get things accomplished are very different the minute you're sitting on the other side of the table as a separate company. People who were your partners and teammates in the old world suddenly have competing priorities. At the highest level of the company, everybody wants the project to go successfully and to happen as smoothly, quickly, and inexpensively as possible, but that doesn't always translate into cooperation through the ranks of a large company.

The Challenge of Differing Speeds

One of the challenges, if your parent company is large, is that large companies have a process for everything. The time it takes them to accomplish tasks can leave you and your team in a constant wait mode. Your team, now that you are a standalone company, will get accustomed very quickly to moving in an agile environment. You and your team will get used to being able to make decisions at lower levels of the organization. This can be an adjustment for those you who are still working with at the legacy firm. You may discover conflict as they enviously look at the autonomy that your team is now operating with, and they may have hidden feelings of resentment.

Escalation

My advice to you about navigating the legacy parent organization, the politics, and the red tape that they put in place, is to not be afraid to escalate when you need to. You are the CTO or CIO of the company now, and technically your peer at the old company is the CTO or CIO of that firm. That's not a card you should often play because it will create animosity and discontent with the people that you need to work with, but recognize that if you keep getting no for an answer, you may need to escalate your requests. Keep the possibility in mind.

Generally, in my experience, everyone is helpful and working towards the same objective—to spin off the company. The advice, coaching, mentoring, and support from the leadership at the legacy firm varies widely from individual to individual and will largely depend on the relationships you had before the sale.

Just remember, if you can't get the support you need in-house, you are not alone. Strategic consultants are out there to help you. CIO networking groups are available to you as well, and social networking platforms can offer you a quick and easy place to get answers to questions. There are plenty of avenues out there for the support you need.

Up Next

Before ending Section 3, we are revisiting communication as it relates to program management. In the next chapter, we examine the importance of regular status updates.

18.

Communicate Program Status

S uccess at spinning off a program of this size is an art in communication, a subject which we've discussed already in previous chapters. The context of communication in this chapter is specifically related to the status of the workstreams and the program itself. You see, it's not just about leading your team to victory. You need to communicate status and progress to all the stakeholders. Stakeholders include anyone with a vested interest in your program: partners, employees, contractors you've hired, executive team, board of directors, and your customers. There are many styles of communication, but the key here is frequency, clarity, transparency, and the consideration of your audience.

You should aim to foster a spirit and culture of no surprises. This is especially true when thinking about what to communicate to the executive team of your firm.

In my experience, a lot of projects report their status as green, usually meaning everything is on track, on budget and there are no expected issues or problems on the horizon that will prevent the team from meeting the expected dates. I think that generally, people are optimistic, and if there are known issues, they feel there is a high probability that they can resolve those issues. Therefore, instead of communicating there are any problems, the project is reported as being on track and on budget.

It's often not until a "showstopper" issue crops up and creates an emergency or a small panic on the team that an issue is reported at all. A showstopper is an issue that is so severe that the team is not able to overcome the hurdle and it will impact the go-live date. A showstopper kind of issue is often related to the timing of a task not fitting into the allotted window, or an assumption on an approach proves to be invalid and there isn't enough time to adjust or change strategies.

As an organization, you and the other leaders need to encourage your teams that it is safe to bring up awareness of issues early. The earlier, the better. In my spin-offs, we always tried to identify risks, meaning potential issues that hadn't occurred yet. If you know something is a risk, you can work to mitigate the risk before it turns into an issue. The idea is to try and embed this type of thinking into the projects. Many people have a fear of delivering bad news. After all, there's a reason the saying, "Don't kill the messenger," exists! It's a metaphor for blaming the person who bears bad news. You want to prevent this fear as much as possible.

If you would like insider advice on how I guided my teams in proactively predicting, reporting, and mitigating risk, I'm available to talk. You will find my contact information on the copyright page.

As the teams get accustomed to bringing up issues early, you, in turn, need to discuss with transparency the issues with other members of your executive team. Communication of the program status to everyone involved is critical. A program dashboard that provides key milestones and status of each workstream is an important tool to help with this communication. As you'll find in the explanation below, once shared with the other executives, this dashboard is something I recommend you share with everyone in the organization.

Communication with the CEO

You should have regular meetings with the chief executive officer of your new organization specifically to discuss the project, your thought processes around vendors selected, and the recommendations you are making. The technology portfolio and projects you are driving are likely to incur a significant amount of the expenses for the first year, so the board will be very interested in the progress, status, issues, and financials.

Meeting with the CEO on a regular basis, and not just for board meeting prep, is important because you'll need that person's support throughout the effort. You might not be reporting to the CEO (it's typical for a CIO/CTO to structurally report to either the chief operating officer or the chief financial officer), but regardless of reporting structure, facetime with the CEO is important. You'll need this sounding board and access to an escalation path if cooperation becomes an issue with the legacy firm.

Other One-on-Ones

In addition to all the audiences mentioned up to this point, you need to have one-on-ones with the senior leaders of all the vendors and strategic partners you have selected in your portfolio. The purpose is two-fold: (1) to understand if you are receiving a consistent message from your respective teams on the status and resolution of issues, and (2) to foster a supporting relationship.

Town Hall-Style Meetings

As suggested earlier, having status meetings with the entire organization, not just the IT group, and sharing the exact program dashboard that you share with other executives, the CEO, and the board of directors will give the employees transparency into the health of the projects. This effort impacts all the employees. Because many are not part of the project themselves, getting them to understand how they are impacted and the timeline for things that are taking place are important parts of organizational change management. If there is a business leader you are partnered with on this effort, I suggest hosting these meetings together.

In my experience, all-employee webinars are a convenient way to deliver updates, but nothing gets your message into the hearts of the organization more than making visits to each physical office and leading a status presentation in the form of a town hall meeting where you can answer questions directly with the people in that location.

SECTION BRIEF

In Section 3, we surveyed all things project management from dividing the whole effort into distinct workstreams to estimating the cost for both the separation effort and the annual expense of IT for running of the new organization. We looked at risk reduction, response to unanticipated issues, and the support you can expect from your parent company.

We ended the section with this chapter on communication: the importance of regular status meetings.

Up Next

Yes, just pulling off the separation itself is a huge task, but that's not all you have on the table! Section 4, "Production Ready," guides you in considering the overall structure, procedures, and processes for the new company after it's been successfully spun off.

We begin section 4 with a chapter on organizational readiness.

PRODUCTION READY

19.

Reach Organizational Readiness

Typically in IT, when we talk about production readiness, we are discussing it in terms of an application or a system. We are evaluating whether a system will function according to the requirements, and we are reviewing test results with the business to determine if the system is ready to go live. That definition certainly applies to this effort. Every application, IT service, and piece of hardware needs to be tested and verified if it's ready.

The biggest lesson from both of my spin-off efforts that I want to share is a type of readiness that is beyond any single application working as expected. It's the concept of organizational readiness. Is your department and the organization *as a whole* ready to be a standalone company?

The OR Workstream

What can be easily lost as an afterthought is actually the most critical workstream in your portfolio: the operational readiness (OR) workstream.

Earlier, I shared that you should have an operational readiness (OR) workstream in your program and assign a dedicated project manager to lead this workstream's effort. The right candidate is someone who is both familiar with IT operations and is an excellent communicator. If you don't have an internal communications department in the organization that will be able to support this person, then the candidate should have strong writing and training skills, and be allowed to hire additional resources to help package information that will be used to train the entire company on the new policies, processes, and tools. The group working in the OR workstream will be defining, documenting, communicating, and educating the entire employee population on the (new) firm's procedures, policies, and instructions for cutover activities.

All companies have policies that set the acceptable methods or behaviors. These are usually introduced to new employees as they join an organization. In a best-practice scenario, they are re-communicated to employees on an annual basis. Employees and contractors should be required to attest that they have read the policy, understand it, and will practice it. The human resources department is usually the driver of this document.

Two Critical Sets of Policies

The handbook may or may not be ready when the IT organization is ready to go live. Keep in mind, there are two critical components from a technology perspective that you will need to drive: security policies and acceptable use policies. My recommendation is that the chief security officer works in partnership with the legal, compliance, and HR departments to draft and roll out these two sets of policies.

To the extent that all the organizational policies are not defined and bundled into an employee handbook, by the time you are ready to launch with some of your new services, your team and the manager you assigned to this program will need to distribute the policies and collect everyone's signed agreement.

The most effective way to roll out new policies is to treat this as employee education and deliver and track completion of the training with an automated training system. If your organization is not ready for that, a PDF with a signature form attesting that the individual has read and understood the policies is all that is needed for protection. This attestation protects the firm in the event anyone violates the policy and the organization is forced to terminate the individual. The organization needs evidence that the person was aware of the policy.

As an aside, I recommend that in today's world with employees spending a significant amount of time at work that your acceptable use policies recognize that some amount of personal use of the corporate resources does occur. A small amount of personal use should be acceptable as long as it does not interfere with work performance and does not expose the organization to any legal liability.

Up Next

IT service management and information technology infrastructure library (ITIL)—the next chapter gives quick summaries of both of these important parts of your production readiness.

20.

Implement IT Service Management and ITIL

There are many books on IT service management and information technology infrastructure library (ITIL). It's not my intention to spend a lot of time on this with you. Instead, I'll to give a quick summary in the event you haven't been involved with this component of IT in the past. My goal is to simplify service management as a practice. In my opinion, the practice and terminology come across as more complicated than they need to.

It took a while for me to grasp that service management is actually quite simple. Here's my simplified explanation of IT service management: there are people who use IT services, and they have a need to make requests, register issues, reset passwords, and monitor the status of their requests. You, as the provider of IT services, have a need to track requests, respond and service those requests, manage all IT assets, and provide access to those assets.

You must also provide a stable and predictable set of services. Each service and asset requires standard maintenance on a planned basis. If the service becomes unstable or unresponsive, your team is responsible for the restoration of the service. This means you bring the service back online and figure out what went wrong, so you can prevent that from happening again.

ITIL is a set of detailed practices for aligning IT service management with the needs of the business. There are different versions of ITIL that have come out over the years, and there are certifications and courses to prepare you and your team in this area if that is a desire. I will share with you just the basics that I think are needed right away.

The implementation of service management in an organization follows a five-step process or life cycle: strategy, design, transition, operations, and continuous improvement.

Service Management Strategy and Design

I recommend the following strategy: implement five basic processes that I consider "must-haves." Once your organization has successfully spun off and is operating in the standalone mode, after ninety days you can review how the processes are supporting the organization to see if improvements are required or if the teams are ready for additional processes to be implemented.

This approach will help you eliminate analysis-paralysis. I want to help you get live. Changes can be made as the organization matures. You need the "right-size" service management processes for your group. These practices can be over-engineered, making it difficult to roll out and implement. My recommendation supports a service management strategy that will get you live, is easy to roll out, will be flexible enough to change as you go, and can be automated quickly for efficiency. If you buy into this strategy, the next step is procedure design.

Although I am not certified in ITIL, I have built from scratch and rolled out service management at two organizations. Here are my recommendations for the five must-have processes. For each of the processes below, I recommend that you name a person responsible for facilitation of the process on an ongoing basis. These people likely all will report to your service desk manager.

1—Service Desk

You should plan on establishing a service desk for employees and possibly for your customers (the need to have an external-facing help desk will depend on the IT services that you provide for that audience). The service desk is the centralized point of the organization for the collection of requests for the purchase, maintenance, and replacement of hardware and software. Your customers, both internal and external, will need to have their passwords reset and be able to request access to equipment and applications. Your team needs to support and fulfill all these requests, and have a predetermined process and expected length of time to complete each type of request.

Since I am assuming that you have hired a service desk manager early in the life cycle of your separation effort, this manager will be critical in establishing the list of requests and determining how each request is fulfilled. Automation and the ability to submit requests without having to call and talk to an individual make for the greatest efficiency. There are tools available to help you automate the processes, although they can be both costly and time-consuming to implement. One of the benefits of deciding to outsource some or all of the service desk to a third party is that they usually have a tool they bring with them for these purposes.

It is essential that even if you outsource this entire function, that you hire an internal service desk manager. After going live, assuming that you have replaced a significant amount of hardware, there will be hundreds of "loose ends" and tickets created by the organization. A manager to handle escalations and to oversee the closing of tickets and the analysis aging tickets is essential for the service of the organization. This role will oversee the service desk managers of the partners you hire and will directly manage the teams fulfilling requests. You will likely have a hybrid model as most firms do.

2—Change Management

Change management is a formal process implemented to track all changes made to your production environment. It includes a process for the entire life cycle of that change, including the request, documentation, testing results, sign-offs, and final approvals that both the change and the environment are ready for deployment. The process should include either a manual or automated way to capture all phases, sign-offs, and required documentation to support the change at each phase. A change management approval board made up of senior IT management should meet on a weekly basis to review all changes that are requested.

Many new organizations and employees complain that change management slows them down and prevents them from being nimble and agile. As the new CIO, you will need to balance this feedback with the risk of having changes that are not reviewed or tested that get moved into production and jeopardize the stability of your platforms and systems. The way that I have kept a nimble and responsive culture in conjunction with a formal tracking and accounting system of changes was to supplement the standard weekly process with an emergency or urgent change request process that only needed electronic approvals.

Ensure the change management process is inclusive of all your strategic partners. Their participation is required for the process to be effective. Asking about change management practices as part of the RFP process and including their compliance as part of the SOW is critical.

3—Incident Management

Incident management is a process established to facilitate communication of production outages and the restoration of service. An incident manager is responsible for working with all service managers to create a list of services, determine the SLAs, document the incident call procedures and call trees, and (typically) initiate a bridge call or conference call where all people who would be involved with the restoration of service dial in. In the initial few minutes of an outage, everyone will focus on impact assessment and how to restore service.

As an organization, you will need to establish some toll gates on how much time should elapse before communicating with both the business leaders and your customers. The rules and the urgency around these toll gates will depend on the business hours of the organization and the criticality of the application experiencing the outage.

4—Problem Management

After service is restored and the systems are running and available, the team will need to identify the root cause of service interruptions. The incident manager should oversee this problem management process, which will include a root cause analysis and documentation of the issues. In addition, the short- and long-term resolutions should be documented to determine if there are systemic stability issues in your portfolio and to identify changes or fixes required to prevent the issue from recurring.

5—Security Access Provisioning and Fulfillment and Inventory Management

This process is responsible for the authorization and termination of access to corporate resources. It is usually performed by a centralized team responsible for provisioning network ids and passwords, email, other corporate communication tools, and access to shared equipment and file shares. Application access is sometimes harder to centralize except in more mature organizations. Having a centralized group improves responsiveness to these tasks and shifts what is less technical work away from your engineers. This function can report to either the chief security officer or the service desk manager.

In my opinion, it is best that the centralized service desk model is separate from your engineering staff where the team members will have a career path that leads from request fulfillment to desktop support and then to service maintenance as an administrator and engineer. These types of career path opportunities will help prevent the high level of turnover that usually occurs within this group. These are typically hourly-paid positions with limited growth potential unless you are focused on building those career paths into your strategy.

As mentioned earlier, the tracking of all assets and hardware and software assignments into an inventory management system is required even if the overall asset management database is not implemented as part of your go live. Excel can be used for the initial rollout and assignments if needed.

Transition, Operations, and Continuous Improvement

Each of the five must-have functions should be clearly documented as a process, and training materials need to be created. You must provide mandatory training sessions for the IT organization on all of the processes. Mandatory training materials and classes should be provided for all the customers of the service desk as well. The full organization needs to understand how to submit a request and identify issues.

The service desk manager will create and review a series of operational reports that help analyze the number of open requests, the aging of outstanding requests, and the ability of the IT organization to meet the established service level agreements and that help facilitate the closure of open incidents and problem management activities.

As already mentioned, a review of the processes on a quarterly basis will help the organization continuously implement improvements as needed.

If you'd like additional information and advice on building and rolling out your service management, then let's have a conversation. I am at your disposal!

Up Next

The final chapter in this section on production readiness addresses the rollout strategy of your workstreams and projects. As you'll recall, I've recommended you do staged rollouts (as opposed to a single "big bang"). The next chapter addresses how to train, talk about, and pull off your various rollouts.

21.

Execute the Production Rollout, Communication, and Training Plans

E arlier, we discussed a "big bang" vs. a staged rollout, and I recommended a staged approach. This chapter on rollout strategies, communication, and training assumes you will follow that approach. As you near the releases of your new IT services, each of them will impact employees. There is a lot of change, and it's all coming quickly in succession. No sooner will one service complete its rollout than you are likely already preparing for the next.

Because the IT managers are busy and preoccupied with operationalizing their services, you will need an independent group of people working on employee communication and training. Don't let this critical component be an afterthought. It's best to think upfront about all the employee touchpoints and what needs to be in this communication strategy.

For a few of the main categories of IT services, I will share a rollout strategy and provide a checklist as a starting point to determine the training and communication needs of the organization. I don't have a recommended order that these services should be rolled out as this will depend on when you and your service providers are ready. However, I will provide a few thoughts on the approach. Also I strongly recommend that your new IT service desk and other must-have service management processes be rolled out in parallel with the first IT service(s).

Service Desk

As the new service desk is being rolled out with the first service, it is operating in parallel with the old service desk. The employees within your organization and those working each of the two service desks need to know which services are supported by whom. Although it sounds complicated, a cheat sheet for everyone is an easy way to accomplish this.

This checklist will get you started on communications concerning this rollout:

- What services are supported by each desk?
- What is the new 800 number?
- How is the self-service request process accessed?
- What are the turnaround times and SLAs for each kind of request?
- How will support be provided? Are there local desktop support teams or will all troubleshooting occur remotely?
- How does the service request ticketing process work?
- What is the escalation process if someone is unable to process business?
- What are the appropriate approval processes and workflows required for purchase and access requests?
- How are inquiries about the status of open tickets made?
- What are the employee onboarding/offboarding workflows?
- How are requests for a transfer of an employee from one department to another done?

Laptops and Desktops

The best approach is to roll out the new machines in waves. Some employees won't use their new devices until the data center conversion is complete. If replacement of employee hardware is required, you may have training and communication needs for all of the following:

- Boot-up process
- Machine login process
- Encryptions software and additional login process and password
- Network ID and password
- Prepping and moving of data
- Mapping of network drives and printers
- Location of resources on the new machine
- New versions of the operating system or desktop software
- Something doesn't work, such as missing data, access issues, trouble-mapping drives, and password resets: how to make a service request

Telephones

I am assuming that you have selected a VOIP (voice over IP) system, which makes the phones dependent on the MPLS and network. The MPLS and network can be rolled out in parallel and sit alongside the parent's network. The network implementation should occur before the phone system. Then after the new phone system is tested, the team can deliver the new phones to each desk. The network connections out to each workstation will be sitting alongside the legacy network.

A parallel service approach does result in a lot of equipment in your data closets, but it reduces risk to bring them up this way. If you are replacing the phone system, there are reasons why having them done in parallel might make sense, but a phone system conversion can occur over a single weekend. This can be executed for all locations at the same time if you have more than one physical location.

I recommend leaving the old system in place during your implementation in case a rollback situation occurs during the cutover weekend. Thirty days later you can come through and remove the old equipment.

If you have replaced the telephony system or if you have company-provided cellphones, you may have training and communication needs for the following:

- Operating the new equipment if you have a new provider or new model
- Setting up expectations for the recording of new in-/out-of-office messages
- Recording a voice mailbox
- Setting up an initial mailbox
- Accessing old voicemails if applicable
- Handling any changes in phone numbers
- Handling the corporate-provided cellphone cutover and conversion process
- Collecting of legacy hardware if applicable
- Making a service request when something doesn't work, such as caller ID problems or the password reset process

Data Center Cutover

Although this workstream typically involves most of the members of your IT organization, it sometimes doesn't always impact the employees except for those involved with the implementation checkout activities. You should try to minimize the impact as much as possible. The data center cutover usually entails copying of all your data from the legacy parent and data center, and transporting over several parallel methods to bring the data up and live on go-live weekend. The applications should be migrated and tested before the cutover.

Here are a few things that may be on your communication list to all employees:

- Information that the transition is happening: dates, timelines, support
- Training on how to access tools and applications if anything has changed
- Instructions to follow if something doesn't work: how to make a service request for any fallout
- Initial morning setup action items if any are identified
- The point person from the business teams for weekend checkout activities
- Checkout/sign-off instructions for weekend checkout teams

Email Conversion

Try to have an email conversion early if possible to get a win under your belt as a team. The complexities depend on the number of domains that are being converted. You can convert email as a big bang or by domain name; each approach has its own benefits. I recommend getting an email conversion team onboard to help you. These consultants are not that expensive and have done hundreds of conversions. Just follow their lead and you will have success.

It's likely you are implementing email in the cloud. Even though ongoing maintenance may be less of a burden for your team, it usually requires desktop instructions and steps that require hands-on desktop attention during the cutover. Your team will need to determine if the process is simple enough to try and communicate the steps to the employees or if you should visit each machine over the conversion period.

Here are the things you might need to communicate to the organization:

- Access to online email boxes
- Setup instructions for desktop software to receive email (i.e., Outlook)
- Setup and access instructions to shared mailboxes
- Steps to find personal PST files, both on individuals' machines and on the file server
- Instructions to follow if something doesn't work: how to make a service request for any fallout, such as missing email boxes, missing PST, access issues to shared mailboxes, and issues with distribution lists
- Location and access of distribution lists or information on changes to lists
- Expectations on when historical data vs. active mailbox conversion will occur

SECTION BRIEF

In this section, we've addressed the key areas you need to prepare for to be considered production ready: IT service management, ITIL, staged rollouts, and communication plans. After the separation, the organization needs to be able to stand on its own, so even with all the work going into the separation effort, you need to carve out time to consider whole operational readiness too. Yes, you've got a lot on your plate, but you have surrounded yourself with experts and supporters, so you can do this and do it well!

I encourage you to contact me too. We can see if it makes sense for me to join your support team, so I can use my experience to ensure you get operational ready. As mentioned in other chapters, you can find my contact information on the copyright page.

Up Next

In the final section, we'll talk about pacing, both for yourself and your team. Don't neglect this issue. Purposefully considering pacing is critical to you and your team in order to avoid burnout so that together you reach the finish line!

PACING

22.

Prevent Burnout

The most important issue to watch out for is the risk of burnout, your personal burnout and that of everyone involved. I know that, in the past, you and your teams have worked on the implementations of applications or systems that have involved Herculean efforts. A spin-off project is similar to executing more than a dozen of these huge implementations *all at the same time*. There is going to be burnout. It's not just a risk; it's a high risk, a looming threat.

To run this marathon effectively and have you and your team make it to the finish line intact is important. In this chapter, I'm sharing a few strategies to help maintain everyone's health and attempt to avoid people giving their notice at a very inconvenient time.

For the Health of Your Team

1. Be honest with your team that this effort is long and hard, and you are worried about everyone pacing themselves.

2. Plan time off for everyone in the department.

3. Announce early on that you will use three-day holiday weekends as potential implementation weekends and that people should not plan travel on that holiday.

4. Schedule at least one three-day weekend per quarter of planned personal time off (PTO) for everyone. Try to get them to sign up ahead of time to orchestrate coverage.

5. Attempt to get people's planned vacations scheduled ASAP. You may need to ask people to move their time off to a different time of the year based on the implementation plans of the workstreams.

6. Insist that your management team does not have overlapping time off, if possible.

7. Schedule fun social events on a regular basis, if not weekly, then biweekly or monthly (i.e., ice cream, pizza, bagels, donuts. IT people like free food!).

For Your Health

1. Heed the age-old advice: "Take care of yourself first." You are in a new role, and there is a lot to learn. Scheduling some downtime might not be possible, but you need to try hard.

2. Hire strategists to give you advice.

3. Carve out time for yourself and your family. A lot of extra time and commitment is required. Set some boundaries. It might be having dinner with your family every night and then working a couple of hours later in the evening. It might be insisting that you make it to church on Sundays. It could be a walk or a run at lunch to clear your head. I recommend you take up meditation. It's amazing how ten minutes in the middle of the day can reduce stress.

4. Get your family's commitment and support that you are working on something that is going to take a lot of time and energy. For a period of time, you won't be as available as you were before.

5. Schedule your family vacation before the first set of services are scheduled to implement. Once the rollouts begin, you won't be taking any time off.

6. Have fun. This opportunity is supposed to be exciting. Try to enjoy the ride.

7. Don't take yourself too seriously. You are going to make mistakes, and you aren't going to handle everything the way you should. You will crack under pressure a few times. Give yourself a break, accept what is, and move on. You are the leader. They are watching you.

8. Walk the talk. If you take a three-day weekend or your family vacation early, then tell everyone that you are doing this to prevent conflict with the project later in the year. In this way, you set the tone for everyone.

SECTION BRIEF

Because pacing yourself and encouraging your team to pace themselves are crucial to the success of the spin-off and to everyone's wellbeing, I recommend you post these health guidelines where you can see them and check in with them daily.

Up Next

In the final chapter of this book, we'll return to the issue of support. As I said at the start, you are not alone. Surround yourself with competent, experienced, and thoughtful experts, so you can get the support you need. This will help you pull off the spin-off better and more smoothly in general, and it will help you personally to avoid burning out.

CONCLUSION

CONCLUSION

23.

Get Support

If you have made it to this part of the book, you might be feeling overwhelmed at the work ahead. Let me remind you that I started off the book by congratulating you. This is a once-in-a-career opportunity. You can make this happen. It will be a success. You can enjoy the process!

The strategies and tips I've shared should allow you a tremendous jumpstart on this effort. Not all spin-off projects are the same, but the two that I was involved with were almost identical. Yes, the vendors were different, our rollout strategies happened in different orders, and the timing of when things were executed was different, but the focus on planning and partners, people, program management, and being production ready were exactly the same.

The need to avoid burning out and to encourage pacing in myself and my team was the same in both as well. Because I've described all these aspects of orchestrating a spin-off in detail, you really should allow yourself to breathe a sigh of relief. With *How to Lead a Corporate Spin-Off* as your companion in this effort, you are not alone.

If you follow my advice and remember to hire strategists and outside consultants to review your approach, help you select partners, and be available to you on a retainer basis throughout the separation project, you will be successful.

You don't have to be alone in this effort. You should make every effort to convince the board and the rest of the executive team that you shouldn't be alone and that you and everyone will benefit when you hire support experts. You won't need to abdicate to the consultants that you hire; instead, use them to learn and avoid their mistakes.

As already mentioned, I am providing videos in the bonus materials that come with the book. You can access these helpful videos at this site: **www.howtoleadacorporatespinoff.com/bonuses.** Again, check the site regularly to find newly added videos and information.

As I've offered already: I too am available to help you in your endeavor in several capacities. Contact me, so we can discuss how I can support you. All my contact information is available on the copyright page.

And again, congratulations on this opportunity! Now go and enjoy it, speed bumps and all!